HUMPBACKS OF HAWAI'I

THE LONG JOURNEY BACK

PAUL H. FORESTELL & GREGORY D. KAUFMAN

ISLAND HERITAGE™
PUBLISHING

Published and distributed by

ISLAND HERITAGE™
P U B L I S H I N G
A DIVISION OF THE MADDEN CORPORATION

94-411 Kō'aki Street, Waipahu, Hawai'i 96797-2806
Orders: (800) 468-2800 • Information: (808) 564-8800
Fax: (808) 564-8877
islandheritage.com

ISBN: 1-59700-743-9
First Edition, First Printing, 2008

To Nancy and Merrill—our compasses, companions,

and courage when life's wind, waves, and current

threaten to throw us off course.

'A'ohe pau ka 'ike i ka halau ho'okahi.

(Knowledge comes from many sources.)

—Mary Kawena Pukui,

'Oleo No'eau: Hawaiian Proverbs and Poetical Sayings

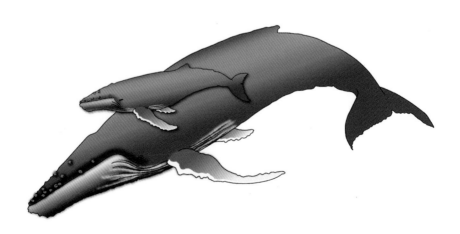

Table of Contents

Foreword

Despite the title, this is not a book entirely about humpback whales. It is a book about adventure, a life-quest, a passion for exploration, voyages around the world, a desire to protect and to teach others to do the same: in short, an ocean odyssey.

The question we each get asked most often is, what got you started in whales? The answer is pretty simple: we are intrigued by the question, what is a whale? We both grew up when the notions that saving whales, saving the earth, and caring about such things as pollution became more critical than they had been for previous generations. Call us "greenies" or blame it on Jacques Cousteau. What has stuck with us from the 1970s is not anarchy or pacifism, but giving a damn about the environment.

One of us grew up near the Pacific coast of Oregon where the four *R*'s (reduce, reuse, return, and recycle) were the norm. The other one of us grew up in Atlantic Canada, where some of the richest fishing grounds in the world have been destroyed by overharvesting. It hardly seems surprising that a fascination with whales and the role they play in our ecosystem would emerge from such beginnings.

What is a whale? We realize we can open up an encyclopedia or dictionary and look up the definition of *whale*, but will the dictionary tell us whether we should care if they all go extinct from rampant hunting? Will it tell us what it is like to look into the eye of a whale, to feel the smoothness of its skin, to see the power and beauty of its graceful movement through the sea? Will it explain our obligation to understand and appreciate the animals and other life-forms with which we share this planet, before sentencing them to extinction?

So we began an odyssey, to discover what Joan McIntyre so eloquently termed "Mind in the Waters." We met in the summer of 1980 when we joined a ragtag group of scientists, sailors, and students on a research project in southeast Alaska. The group's mission was to address a variety of questions pertaining to the impact of human activities on humpback whales. One question in particular was, why, all of a sudden, were they abandoning preferred feeding grounds in Glacier Bay? Was it the burgeoning cruise ship industry? Was it increased ocean noise (newly recognized as a form of pollution)? Was it due to El Niño (a phenomenon little understood at that time)? Was it because of overfishing? Did oil exploration have some hand in the matter?

That summer in southeast Alaska changed both of our lives: partly because of the excitement of discovery (this was the first time coordinated feeding among large groups of humpback whales was observed at close range, and it was also the first time the fascinating feeding sounds associated with such groups were recorded), but mostly because this was an adventure that led to a deep friendship that has continued to this day. Friendship actually sounds simplistic; compadres, sidekicks, covisionaries seems more like it. One need only imagine two guys drawn from totally different backgrounds, dropped on an isolated rock in southeast Alaska, several hundred miles from any real civilization, to realize you either collaborate or shoot each other.

From an inauspicious beginning of playing "Stratego" on the helipad of a coast guard lighthouse station through long Alaskan summer evenings, we have since traveled to areas of the world and parts of the ocean others only dream about. From the remote islands of Ogasawara, Japan, to the Great Barrier Reef of Australia, from watching humpbacks cavort near the equator off Ecuador, to observing the largest group of humpbacks we have ever seen (thirty-six) off Maui; from Canada to Costa Rica, Tonga, New Zealand, American Samoa, and Mexico, we have traveled the Pacific Ocean on a shoestring

in pursuit of knowledge and understanding with our friendship and a common purpose to sustain us.

This book is written by not one, but two authors with two voices, two personalities, and two perspectives. We are sons of different mothers, from distinctly different backgrounds. One is a Canadian now living in New York, and the other a native of Oregon who has lived for more than three decades on Maui. As you read what we have written, you will generally be hard-pressed to differentiate one voice from the other—but listen closely and you may hear our different perspectives shine through our common excitement.

This book is unique not just because of the facts we present, but because we have lived the adventures and discovery behind many of the facts. What we have seen with our own eyes deserves to be shared, told to the public, and not just buried in a scientific journal on some dusty academic shelf. Our journey has been exciting, challenging, and humbling. We have never lost our fascination or respect for the humpback whale. It is with this insatiable enthusiasm that we share this book with you.

Greg Kaufman (L) and Paul Forestell (R), shown here on Maui in 1995, have studied humpback whales together throughout the North and South Pacific for three decades.

Why We Wrote This Book

For more than thirty years we have dedicated ourselves to sharing information with the public that is factual, interesting, and based on firsthand observation. This book was written and then written again in response to the many requests we have received for information about humpback whales. There are now many books about whales and dolphins that have been published, prompted by an ever-increasing public awareness of the fragility of our marine resources. None of these describe the latest discoveries or interesting field observations experienced firsthand by the researchers themselves, nor do they suit the needs of those with a special interest in Hawai'i's humpback whales. Books currently available simply summarize the

available literature, are too general, or concentrate on details too specialized for the layperson. Often they are field guides that provide isolated facts about species that most of us will never see. We believe the average person interested in Hawai'i's humpback whales wants to know what humpback whales are, why they come to Hawai'i, what they do while they are here, where they can be seen, the most effective ways to observe them, and most important, if they are recovering from years of exploitation.

In 1986 we published our first field guide to humpback whales in Hawai'i. Since that time new knowledge has emerged, and we have traveled the Pacific studying humpback whales in a wide range of habitats. New scientific discoveries, combined with our increased experience and exposure, have convinced us that a

Humpback whales are the most approachable and entertaining of the great whales, drawing millions of people from all over the world to learn about their curious behaviors.

new and substantially revised book is now needed.

Humpback whales have been a focus of scientific study in Hawai'i since 1975. We have been a part of this adventure from its beginning. This compendium highlights our own field studies, our interactions with colleagues, and our understanding of historically important and currently popular theories of the biology and behavior of humpbacks and the other great whales. We remain committed to providing you, the reader, an opportunity to learn about one species of whale in sufficient degree to be able recognize its behaviors and displays, and perhaps even to interpret the significance of many of them. We trust this second book will continue our tradition of making whalewatching both an exciting and educational opportunity.

This book is more than a simple whalewatching guide. Even if you never visit Hawai'i or see a humpback in its ocean home, we provide an informative and richly illustrated description of the humpback whale and its behavior. This book has been written for a large but select audience: those who, like us, harbor a special fascination for this curious, knobby-headed creature with the haunting song and artful aerobatics. To ensure their survival, those of us who have an interest in watching humpback whales should become educated about their nature and habits before imposing on their life and activities, just as we might educate ourselves about the language and culture of another country before visiting it.

Acknowledgments

We recognize the contributions of many in the development of the ideas found on the following pages. A full and accurate list of the specific individuals who have contributed to our knowledge and efforts is impossible. Our teachers, mentors, colleagues, and collaborators form a large and diverse network. Some would be upset if we forgot to mention them, and others would probably be upset if we presumed to include them!

Many of the beautiful photographs were submitted by our supporters following whalewatching trips with Pacific Whale Foundation Eco Adventures. We also extend our deep appreciation to Monica and Michael Sweet and Bryant Austin. We feel our greatest sense of obligation is to our 'ohana—the Pacific Whale Foundation's enthusiastic supporters and dedicated staff, and our understanding families. To all those who have helped us learn about the humpback whale, and who have encouraged and supported us in our research efforts over the years, we hope this book will convince you that the help was well placed.

Overview

Recreational excursions to view marine mammals are among the most visible, accessible, and frequent of human activities in the marine environment. Whale and dolphin watching is one of the world's fastest-growing sectors of marine tourism. The explosion of interest in whales and dolphins has been a remarkable phenomenon. The transition from whale killing to whalewatching has galvanized the interest of nations around the world. A concern for the welfare of whales and dolphins has joined people from all corners of the earth in a common front that transcends culture, race, and politics.

Before the 1970s most of what was known about whales came from the observations of biologists working on board whaling ships, or at the shore-

based whaling stations that once dotted the coasts of many nations. Much of this work was directed toward more efficient commercial exploitation of what was regarded by many as an endless resource. Throughout the first half of the twentieth century, biologists were hard at work discovering where new whale stocks could be found, and patterns of individual birth rates, growth rates, and life expectancy. Starting in the late 1950s, and throughout the 1960s and 1970s, a small number of scientists began studying the behavior of live marine mammals, both in the open ocean and in oceanariums, where smaller whales and dolphins could be maintained for extended periods. In response to the increasing sensitivity of both the scientific community and the public to the plight of marine mammals, new techniques for studying them were developed. Hydrophones (underwater microphones) and cameras displaced the harpoon and rendering tank. Where once biologists accompanied huge oceangoing whaling factories to the polar seas, researchers now set out in small sailing yachts and fragile inflatable outboard boats to view these living animals close at hand. New techniques for identifying whales and their sex, for recording and classifying their sounds and behaviors, for assessing their population status and movement patterns, and for studying their social interactions have been developed and improved during the past fifty years.

Importantly, none of the new techniques require that the subjects of the study be dead upon the slipway of a factory ship or shore-whaling station. To this day there remains no justification for killing whales to understand them.

Our story of the North Pacific humpback whale begins with a description of its general biological characteristics. We then discuss the natural history of the humpback—characteristics of its evolution and anatomy, and the nature of its adaptations to an ocean existence. This sets the stage for a description of humpback whale behaviors, which includes a behavior guide and an explanation of the contexts in which these behaviors are seen. Having read this material, a whalewatcher will have a real sense of what whale behaviors they're observing. We then consider the activities that humpback whales engage in during their residence in Hawai'i. Next we talk about their current status and future prospects for a full recovery, and the importance of our education in ensuring that recovery. The final sections provide hints on how to select a responsible whalewatch, tips for getting the most out of your whalewatching experience, and best practices to avoid disturbing whales while watching them.

During the three decades we have observed humpback whales throughout the Pacific, we have felt a profound commitment to make our findings (and the findings of other researchers) accessible to the public. While we recognize that data is useless if it doesn't make its way into scientific publications, we would add that data is also useless if it simply sits on the library shelf. The supporters we have met while on whalewatching expeditions have funded most of our research. Literally millions of people have learned about whales through our efforts, and we take pride in knowing that we have been at the forefront of educating the public, from a scientific perspective, about whales and the watery world in which they live.

Section I

THE NATURAL LIFE OF HUMPBACK WHALES

Chapter 1

VISITORS TO PARADISE

The Kumulipo, a sacred ancient chant, recounts the Hawaiian story of earth's creation. The ocean and its creatures and the land and its creatures all grew out of an initial formation of coral. Twenty-nine pairs of fish were created, each with a corresponding land plant to act as guardian. The largest of the fish was the *palaoa* (whale), whose guardian on land was the *'aoa* (sandalwood tree). *Hanau ka palaoa noho i kai . . . Kia'i 'ia e ka 'aoa"* reads the Kumulipo (The whale is born into the sea . . . Protected by the sandalwood).

The pairing of *palaoa* and *'aoa* as charge and guardian has both poetry and irony to it. The sandalwood, once prolific on the slopes of Hawai'i Island, made its presence known by its pungent aroma, which was noticed even by sailors many

miles offshore. Similarly, the hauntingly beautiful chorus of the humpback whale song during the annual sojourn in Hawai'i could be heard through the wooden hulls of visiting ships.

The sandalwood was harvested in great and uncontrolled amounts and traded for goods and currency immediately following contact with Europeans. Years later, in the absence of its ancient guardian, the humpback suffered a similar fate in the North Pacific. Since 1992 increasingly successful efforts have been undertaken to reintroduce sandalwood trees on the island of Maui. As a result of both private and government efforts, thousands of native 'aoa are now growing in areas like Kahakulao on Maui's north shore, forest reserves throughout the island, and even along the Lahaina Pali Trail. In a similar fashion, agencies and individuals have collaborated to focus world attention on education and conservation efforts to prevent the extinction of the humpback. We have played a significant role in that

partnership, and Hawai'i has been ground zero for focusing the world's attention on the importance of saving the humpback whale. While it is sad to note that in Hawai'i today both the *palaoa* and the 'aoa remain endangered, we take hope and solace in the efforts of visionary Hawaiians on the one hand, and a vast army of whale supporters throughout the world on the other, that both species will return from the brink of extinction.

The Hawaiian archipelago is a fifteen-hundred-mile-long chain of nineteen islands and small atolls and numerous shoals and reefs, which stretch along a thin, northwesterly line across the middle of the North Pacific. The archipelago is the most isolated group of islands in the world, situated almost directly in the middle of the Pacific basin. It is approximately three thousand miles south of Alaska and twenty-four hundred miles west of California. Just north of Midway Islands, near the extreme northwesterly tip of the archipelago, a string of spectacular

seamounts representing the submerged remnants of earlier islands stretches northward almost to the Aleutian Islands. The main island chain that comprises the present-day landmass of Hawai'i developed from twenty-five million years of volcanic activity in the southernmost area of Hawai'i Island, from which the archipelago derives its name. Following its creation, each new island moved inexorably northwestward with the shifting crustal plate on which the erupted volcanic land masses sit. Even today, a new island is being formed roughly twenty miles south of Hawai'i Island where Lō'ihi seamount rises some two and a half miles from the seafloor. With more than a mile to go, it will not break the surface for more than a thousand years.

The inhabited islands are found in the southernmost portion of the chain and include Kaua'i, O'ahu, Moloka'i, Lāna'i, Maui, and Hawai'i. The smaller islands of Ni'ihau (just west of Kaua'i) and Kaho'olawe (off the southwest end of Maui) complete the area most generally referred to as the main Hawaiian Islands. Beyond Kaua'i the northwest Hawaiian Islands extend over

twelve hundred miles to Kure Atoll. This relatively pristine area is the primary habitat of the highly endangered Hawaiian monk seal, endemic to the islands. The area was designated the largest marine conservation area in the world in June 2007. Named the Papahānaumokuā kea (*Pa-pa-ha'-now-mo-kooa-kaya*) Marine National Monument, it is now under consideration as a world heritage site. The name for the monument, chosen by an advisory council of native Hawaiians, refers to the mythical sacred birthplace of all life, to which the spirits return after death.

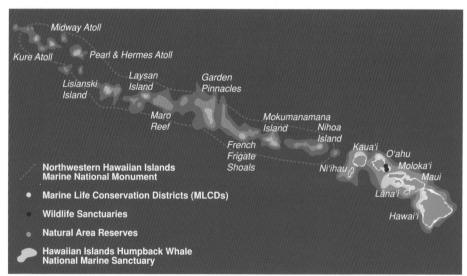

The Hawaiian archipelago, the most isolated islands in the world, stretch from Hawai'i Island (to the south east) fifteen hundred miles northwest to Kure Atoll.

A relatively shallow underwater shelf, less than six hundred feet deep, surrounds each of the main islands. For the most part, the surrounding shelf extends only two or three miles offshore and then drops precipitously to oceanic depths of more than twelve thousand feet. A major exception is found in the area of the four-island group, comprised of Moloka'i, Lāna'i, Maui, and Kaho'olawe. Here the six-hundred-foot-deep contour encompasses a broad, irregularly shaped shelf on which the four islands sit, and includes Penguin Bank extending off the southwest coast of Moloka'i. Penguin Bank is a twenty-seven-mile-long, ten-mile-wide shelf ranging in depth from 150 to 300 feet. It creates an area of upwelling that once was capable of supporting a major bottom-fishery.

Each year, increasing numbers of visitors (nearly 7.5 million in 2007) flow in and out of the islands of Hawai'i, drawn here by the tropical climate, white sand beaches, and *aloha* spirit of island residents. Humans are not the only regular visitors to these waters. Each winter the Hawaiian Islands play host to a celebrity of sufficient distinction to have had the only national marine sanctuary in the country designated in its honor. While not anywhere near as numerous as the humans who come to Hawai'i, the humpback whales' annual arrival nonetheless generates considerable excitement and interest.

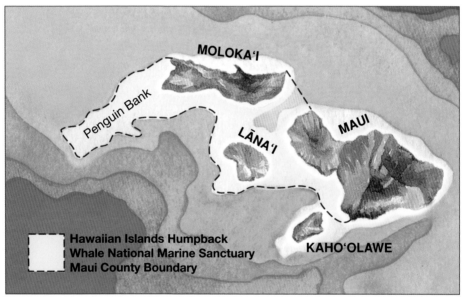

The Four Island Area (comprised of Moloka'i, Maui, Kaho'olawe and Lāna'i) sits on a large and irregularly shaped shelf that provides relatively shallow (less than 600 feet) habitat where large numbers of migrating humpback whales congregate during the winter breeding season.

Chapter 2
THE KOHOLĀ IN HAWAI'I

In spite of the fact that the humpback whale is, in current times, a regular and highly visible visitor to these waters, the search to understand their importance in the cultural and economic history of ancient Hawaiians continues. Various species of toothed whales, called *palaoa* by the Hawaiians, were familiar to local inhabitants and became a part of their legends and intricate systems of taboos. Elaborate *lei* (*niho lei palaoa; whale tooth necklace*) made with strands of human hair and whale teeth

became sacred artifacts among Hawaiian royalty. They were believed to represent godly strength and were a mark of high rank. Many place names throughout the islands include the name for the toothed whale, *palaoa*. Palaoa Point on the south end of Lāna'i has what appears to be an ancient petroglyph, or rock drawing, of a man riding on the back of a whale. There is a Hawaiian legend that tells of a priest's son taken off to the spirit world on the back of a whale. One of the places where we used to launch our research

boat, off the east end of Lāna'i, is called Halepalaoa (whale house). On Hawai'i Island near Hilo an ancient temple called Kaipalaoa (sea of the whale), was a favored gathering place for royalty. A number of other locations throughout the islands, such as Kukuipalaoa (whale lamp), off the north coast of Moloka'i, pay tribute to the presence and importance of toothed whales.

While toothed whales were of substantial cultural importance to the Hawaiians, the significance of the humpback, a baleen whale, is much less clear. In modern times, the Hawaiian word *koholā* has been used to refer to the humpback. *Koholā* appears to have been derived from the Tongan word for whale (*tofua'a*). How *koholā* came only to refer to the humpback whale remains a matter of conjecture. There are a number of place names throughout the Hawaiian Islands incorporating references to *koholā*. These include Koholālele (leaping whale), a fishpond on O'ahu; Lae O Na Koholā, (cape of whales) on Kaho'olawe; and Pu'ukoholā (whale point) Heiau on Hawai'i Island. The latter location is a massive temple built by Kamehameha I on the premise that if he did so he would become the supreme ruler of the Hawaiian Islands.

It seems paradoxical that an event as significant as the annual arrival of humpback whales would have such little apparent salience in the legends and stories of ancient Hawai'i. One possibility is that the whales were so significant that they were regarded by some as *'aumakua* (the souls of departed ancestors). Perhaps in order to protect their *'aumakua*, little information about the humpback whales was shared with others, particularly the European and American whalers intent on killing them. This could also explain the lack of evidence that Hawaiians hunted humpbacks before the nineteenth century.

Whaling ships arrived in Hawai'i

A contemporary drawing of Waimea village on Hawai'i Island shows what island life looked like when whalers first arrived during the early part of the 19th century.

during the first quarter of the nineteenth century, when the *Balaena* from New Bedford and the *Equator* from Nantucket anchored off Hawai'i Island in 1819. A few years later the whalers discovered that the nearshore waters off Lahaina and Honolulu were more hospitable and provided a safer anchorage. These whalers were not looking for humpbacks but were on their way from the Offshore Ground, between Peru and Hawai'i, to the Japan Ground to the northwest—both areas where sperm whales could be found in large numbers. Honolulu and Lahaina were roadsteads, often for hundreds of ships at a time. Upwards of five hundred ships a year would pay harbor fees, a surcharge for the lighthouse, and purchase fresh water, creating substantial income for these ports. Hawaiian ports were also great sources of temptation for the desperate sailors who had been cramped into tight-fitting, foul-smelling quarters for many months at a time. Native Hawaiians were often recruited by captains desperate to replace sailors who had abandoned ship or were killed in the often wild activities while the ships were in port.

In his 1840 book, *Two Years Before The Mast*, Richard Dana speaks highly of the *kanaka* (Hawaiian) sailors he met, calling them the most sensitive and trustworthy he knew, and claiming he would far quicker approach a Hawaiian when in need than one of his fellow Americans.

The presence of the whaling ships led to a shore-based whale fishery between 1840 and 1870, and the promise of humpback whales in great numbers was used in an attempt to lure whaling ships from Honolulu to Lahaina in 1856. By the late 1860s there were up to five shore-based whaling stations in operation, but success at taking humpbacks was so sporadic that each capture was sufficient to warrant a full-blown account in the local papers. The method was to set out after a mother and calf, harpoon the calf as quickly as possible to keep the mother close by, and then lance the mother repeatedly until she bled to death. The price of oil rendered from humpback blubber was much lower than that of the more highly regarded sperm whale oil. The humpbacks, which fast while in Hawaiian waters, generally gave little return for the effort required to bring them ashore. It is little surprise, therefore, that the shore-based whaling stations were a relatively unsuccessful and short-lived enterprise.

Throughout the end of the nineteenth century and the beginning of the twentieth century, humpbacks were of little interest in Hawai'i. Along the West Coast of the mainland and throughout much of their Alaskan feeding area, however, they were hunted intensively. Until the mid-1970s there were only two periods during which whales received any attention in Hawai'i: during World War II they were used for target practice by bombers, and in the 1950s an O'ahu-based whalewatching group formed, which observed small numbers of whales in the O'ahu area of Koko Head. Little notice seems to have been paid to the humpbacks otherwise.

Then in 1977 James Hudnall, a freelance photographer and self-styled researcher, wrote in *Audubon* magazine of swimming with humpback whales just off Maui. Diving from a small boat with no more equipment than a mask, fins, snorkel, and an underwater camera, Hudnall provided a dramatic glimpse of living whales. He described them as incredibly gentle and approachable and provided the spectacular images to prove it. Two years later a *National Geographic* film (The Great Whales) repeated the message. By that time tourists on Maui were already showing increased interest in whalewatching, which had just begun to develop.

When Pacific Whale Foundation began whalewatching in 1980, no more than twenty-five thousand people went on dedicated whalewatching excursions. Today more than three hundred twenty-five thousand flock to Hawai'i each year for the express purpose of seeing whales in the wild.

Chapter 3
WHAT IS A WHALE?

Most people who see whales in the wild get a great deal of satisfaction and excitement from the experience, but it is clear that few really understand what a humpback whale is and how it differs from other mammals, other inhabitants of the ocean, or other whales. In order to develop an accurate perception of the humpback whale, it is necessary to place it in the context of the general group of marine mammals known as cetaceans.

Whales, dolphins, and porpoises are collectively called cetaceans, after the Latin *cetus*, related to the Greek word for sea monster (*ketos*). Cetaceans have intrigued humans for centuries. As early as 400 BCE, Aristotle taught and wrote about whales, dolphins, and porpoises. In *Historia Animalium*, a book detailing all the different animal forms he knew about, Aristotle noted that cetaceans were closely related to other viviparous (literally, live-bearing, as opposed to oviparous, or egg-bearing), warm-blooded species that breathe through lungs. He pointed out that cetacean mothers nurse their young through mammary glands, and that individuals communicate underwater using a wide range of sounds. He described their sensory systems and told of fishermen driving herds of dolphins ashore by terrifying them with sound. He gave rather accurate information about the life expectancy of dolphins (twenty to thirty years) based on observations of individuals whose tail flukes had been marked with notches by fishermen.

While Aristotle differentiated cetaceans from fish, birds, and terrestrial animals like humans, he also wrestled with the issue

Dolphins are toothed cetaceans (odontocetes), and while related to baleen whales (mysticetes) such as the humpback, they exhibit very different social and migratory patterns.

of classification, noting that cetaceans could neither be considered truly terrestrial (taking in air) nor truly aquatic (taking in water), for in his view they did both: taking in air and water and then expelling both through the blowholes. Because of their dependence on an aquatic habitat, cetaceans were generally classified with fish until the initiation of structurally based taxonomic systems in the seventeenth century. These eventually led to the famous binomial system of Carl Linnaeus in the late 1700s, which is still in use today.

Cetaceans are now classified as mammals. Taxonomically they are distinguished from other mammals on the basis of a set of five characteristic features pertaining to specializations of the skull, inner ear, and tooth structures. Cetaceans are one of three orders of mammals that contain marine (ocean-living) species. The other two orders in which marine mammals are found are Carnivora, which includes many terrestrial species as well as marine-dwelling polar bears, sea otters, and pinnipeds (walruses, seals, fur seals, and sea lions); and Sirenia, which includes manatees, dugongs, and the first species of marine mammal known to have been driven into extinction by humans—Steller's sea cow. Cetaceans and sirenians are the only mammals to live their entire lives in the water. Relative to the marine mammals of the order Carnivora (polar bears, sea otters, and pinnipeds), cetaceans and sirenians appeared at a much earlier evolutionary time—the earliest fossil evidence suggests that cetacean ancestors were busy trying to figure out how to make a living in the ocean nearly fifty-five million years ago.

While current textbooks report that there are eighty-three species of living cetaceans, there is not yet complete agreement on the exact number, and new species continue to be found. There have been as many as fourteen cetacean species identified in the last one hundred years, with at least three new

In addition to whales and dolphins, Hawai'i is also home to the only endemic (native) marine mammal found there, the Hawaiian Monk seal.

species named in the past decade or so. Taxonomists frequently disagree on the classification of specimens (which may include fossilized material from extinct animals, remnants of skeletal material from currently extant but dead animals, or well-documented observations of living animals). Arguments may be presented for considering a given specimen or observation as evidence of a separate species, for designating it as a variant form of an already named species, or for creating a subspecies category. There are also disagreements about what Latin names should take precedence when a new species is determined, and changes in both genus and species names are an ongoing occurrence.

Scientists from New Zealand and the United States recently reexamined five specimens of whales that stranded on the California coast between 1975 and 1997, and concluded there was sufficient evidence to designate a new species. They named it *Mesoplodon perrini* after Dr. W. F. Perrin, an American cetacean biologist widely known for his efforts in science and conservation.

In the summer of 2002, while we were undertaking humpback whale research off the coast of Ecuador, we were shown a cleaned skeleton of an eleven-foot whale that had beached itself some six months earlier, to be discovered soon after by friends who run a small beachside hotel. The carcass was reportedly in rather good condition when it was first discovered, although the teeth, dorsal fin, and edges of the tail flukes had been removed. It appeared the whale may have been caught in a fishing net, and whoever found it removed the teeth as souvenirs and cut the dorsal fin and tail flukes to sell as shark fins. When we showed our friends a field guide of marine mammals, they emphatically declared their find to be identical with a drawing of the Peruvian beaked whale (*Mesoplodon peruvianus*), first identified as a species in 1991. This species has only been observed in the wild in Peru on five or six occasions, and our friends' find is the first time its occurrence has been reported in Ecuador. It seemed especially sad to see such a rare creature come to such an ignominious end.

In theory, species characterization is based on an examination of heritable characteristics, which may be demonstrated as structural or physiological features, genetic markers, or behavioral traits. Since behaviors don't fossilize and molecular techniques are relatively new, species determination over the past two hundred years has been based primarily on morphometric (structural and physiological) features and the phylogenetic (evolutionary relationships) patterns of species that share similar features. Recent advances in molecular techniques, however, have revolutionized interpretations of the evolution and classification of cetacean species, the genetic relationships among those species, and the patterns in which given species radiated, or spread out, during evolutionary history across the world's oceans.

Located within the cytoplasm surrounding the nucleus of each cell of an animal are many hundreds of tiny organelles, or bodies, called mitochondria that control the energy production of the cell. Like the nucleus, mitochondria contain DNA, a molecule that occurs in one of four base forms that can be strung together in complementary pairs of unique sequences to form genes and chromosomes. While any given gene in the nucleus only has two copies (one on each chromosome, with one chromosome inherited from each parent), however, there may be thousands of copies of mitochondrial (*mt*) genes in each cell's cytoplasm. Interestingly, while nuclear DNA is inherited from both parents, *mt*DNA appears to only come from the mother, so there is only one genetic blueprint in the mitochondria that gets copied multiple times.

Mitochondria have a fascinating evolutionary history. They are believed to have been ancient forms of free-living bacteria, which were taken up millions of years ago by early types of animal cells through a kind of symbiotic process. As millennia passed, many of the genetic capabilities of the mitochondria were taken over by the cell, and the genetic complement of the mitochondria became much reduced. In humans there are only thirty-seven genes encoded in the *mt*DNA. In addition, on each copy of the DNA sequence within the mitochondria, a region that controls the ongoing manufacture of *mt*DNA is approximately ten times more likely than nuclear DNA to develop aberrations or mutations. Many of these changes occur within the life of the organism, and may be responsible for the effects of aging. These so-called somatic variations are not heritable. Other mutations occur during formation of the egg, however, and are passed on by a mother to her offspring. Since this control region of *mt*DNA does not function as a gene, its mutations are less likely than genetic mutations to be changed through natural selection operating on successive generations. Consequently, inherited changes in the control region of *mt*DNA remain for endless generations, creating a kind of molecular scrapbook of an individual's maternal lineage and evolutionary history. Mitochondrial DNA has been considered an ideal source of information about species relationships and evolutionary connections because it is highly susceptible to heritable variations, is relatively easy to obtain, can be readily copied, and is simpler to interpret because it only follows the lineage of one parent (the mother).

Molecular biologists have developed a sophisticated series of protocols for extracting DNA from cellular material, then amplifying (replicating) it and modifying it in various ways to read the sequences in order to compare samples from different specimens. This can allow some incredibly powerful analytical capabilities. By comparing *mt*DNA samples from two or more specimens, scientists can determine with reasonable degrees of certainty whether the specimens came from the same individual, individuals from the same population, or from the same species; or whether different species are related, and if so, how closely. This has led to a considerable ongoing effort to reassess the taxonomy and evolution of cetacean species. Sometimes the morphological and molecular data agree, but more often than not it seems to disagree. In order to address a variety of potential difficulties with using only *mt*DNA markers to study relationships between organisms, scientists have also developed techniques that examine variations in nuclear DNA markers found on portions of DNA strands called microsatellites (relatively short sections of repeating sequences on a strand) and minisatellites (longer sections of repeating sequences), variations in the Y chromosome (found only in males, and therefore only passed on by fathers to sons), and a number of noncoding segments both outside of and within genes.

Genetic analysis of humpback whale populations throughout the world have to date confirmed that there is one species worldwide. It is clear, however, that the worldwide distribution of humpback whales is based on a number of discrete subpopulations. The greater the physical distance between the subpopulations,

Relative sizes of the smallest dolphin (Hectors dolphin), human, orca, humpback whale and blue whale (the largest animal ever to inhabit the earth).

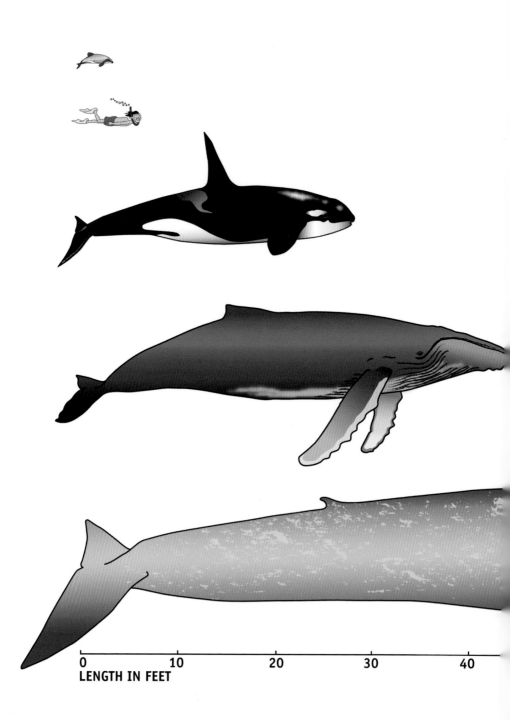

LENGTH IN FEET

0   10   20   30   40

the greater the diversity of their genetic difference. While interchange between contiguous populations may occur on a limited basis, it appears that humpback whales generally maintain breeding and feeding site fidelity.

Hawaiian humpback whales are a distinct subpopulation that breed in areas throughout the Hawaiian archipelago and feed primarily in southeast Alaska. Both genetic and photo-ID data show evidence of limited interchange with both the western and eastern North Pacific subpopulations, though it is not clear where or when during migration such interchange takes place.

The results of genetic analysis of cetacean speciation are ongoing, and have raised many questions about the number and classification of species. Currently, we can only say with any certainty that there are eighty to eighty-five species of whales, dolphins, and porpoises. The exact number depends on resolving the many arguments that have arisen as modern-day molecular techniques challenge the morphometric conclusions of the past two centuries. The various species we do know about range in size from the relatively small four-foot Hector's dolphin of New Zealand to the largest animal ever to live, the one-hundred-foot blue whale, found in all oceans of the world.

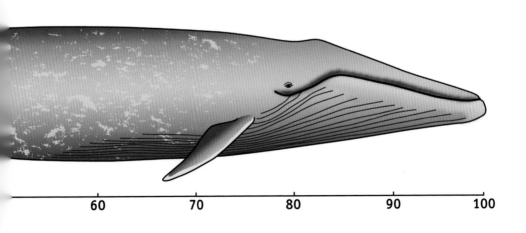

60   70   80   90   100

Chapter 4

ADAPTING TO LIFE BENEATH THE SEA

I t is generally accepted that land mammals were the precursors of modern cetaceans. Modern whales, dolphins, and porpoises are generally defined as totally aquatic swimmers, with relatively streamlined bodies lacking hind limbs, a specialized tail for propulsion, forelimbs shaped as flippers that serve as paddles, little or no hair, and an insulating layer of blubber. The bodies of whales, dolphins, and porpoises have undergone many adaptive changes to meet the demands of an aquatic environment. As they evolved during the last fifty to fifty-five million years, cetaceans in general have had to face the challenge of acquiring mechanisms and behaviors that would facilitate the transition from land to sea. Intense demands were placed on finding new ways to deal with the problems of mobility, sensory perception, thermoregulation, respiration, orientation and balance, communication, nutrition, water and salt balance, avoidance of predators, courting, mating, giving birth, rearing offspring, and resting.

Cetaceans emerged as a distinct marine mammal form during the Eocene

Cetaceans have had to develop many anatomical, physiological and behavioral adaptations during their 55-million year transition from terrestrial to marine existence.

epoch, which spanned some sixteen million years, beginning about fifty-four million years ago. The cetaceans most probably developed from a line of terrestrial mammals called condylarths that spread throughout much of the world during the Paleocene epoch, following the extinction of dinosaurs some sixty-five million years ago. The loss of the dinosaurs opened a huge niche for new mammalian forms to fill, resulting in many lines of development among the condylarths, including the modern-day ungulates (hoofed mammals, which include the artiodactyls, with an even number of hooves, and the perissodactyls, with an odd number). The earliest cetacean ancestors (known as archaeocetes) were four-legged mammals that inhabited coastal areas and developed the capability to swim in rivers and the nearshore ocean. Their connection with modern-day cetaceans is that they contained the structural features in the skull, inner ear, and teeth still found in today's cetaceans, even though their body shape, habitat, diet, and behavior were very different. Some archaeocete fossils show positioning of the nostrils midway between those of their earlier ancestors and modern day cetaceans.

The earliest condylarths (from which the ungulates evolved) were herbivores, but there eventually evolved a line of carnivorous mammals within a group known as the mesonychid condylarths. Until recently the dominant view was that cetaceans evolved from the mesonychids. Following the recent analysis of fossil evidence discovered at two different sites in Pakistan, however, it has been demonstrated that cetaceans evolved from the artiodactyls (modern species in this group include cattle, deer, camel, hippopotamus, sheep, and goat), not the mesonychid condylarths. Two independent teams of scientists looking at the ankle bones of four newly discovered species of archaeocetes found structural evidence that linked these early whales more closely to artiodactyls than mesonychids. Recent evidence suggests whales originated from a type of common aquatic artiodactyl that also gave rise to the South Asian Raoellidae family. The raoellids, now extinct, were therefore a sister group to whales. It is believed that the closest relative of whales living today is their more distantly related "cousin" the hippopotamus, which shares a much older, and as yet, unknown common ancestor.

As they continued to explore the rivers and estuaries in search of a more hospitable ecosystem throughout the Eocene and early Oligocene epochs, archaeocetes further developed the unique anatomy that distinguishes them from land animals. To facilitate breathing while in the water, the nostrils literally migrated toward the top and back of the head, and the skull and braincase became massively foreshortened, or telescoped, in order to accommodate the change. The neck became nearly indistinguishable from the remainder of the body, which began to elongate. The forelimbs became paddle shaped, the hind limbs began to shrink, and the tail grew into a functional propulsion and steering mechanism. The mouth, too, became more suited to seizing fish. Cetaceans may have emerged following a major change in dietary needs and dental structure. This was apparently followed by further changes in the skull to accommodate sensory processes associated with echolocation.

An artist's rendition of a small, deer-like, plant-eating, marine artiodactyl named Inohydus, which lived 48 million years ago. Scientists have suggested this may be an early ancestor of today's cetaceans.

The oldest known archaeocete, *Himalayacetus subathuensis*, has been identified recently from a jawbone and teeth found in the Himalayas, dating from about fifty-four million years ago. It was a ten-foot-long, seal-like animal that may have spent part of its life on land. Another primitive cetacean, *Pakicetus inachus*, was discovered in the Himalayan region of Pakistan, where it was deposited nearly fifty million years ago. Although *Pakicetus* may have lived both on land and in the water along rivers and estuaries, its skull shows the specializations in dentition associated with cetacean dietary preferences and the inner ear structure that facilitated underwater hearing.

The archaeocetes flourished throughout the early and middle Eocene, and lasted through the Oligocene, until about thirty million years ago. There were as many as 140 genera (groups of species) of archaeocetes, compared to 40 genera of modern cetaceans. As the archaeocetes became extinct, two other suborders of cetaceans evolved, both of which survive today (although many species that evolved within the two suborders over the past thirty-five million years have gone extinct). The two modern suborders of cetaceans are the Mysticeti ("mustached

sea monsters") and Odontoceti ("toothed sea monsters"). The earliest fossil evidence for humpback whales comes from Florida and Canada and dates back to the late Pleistocene epoch, less than half a million years ago.

Although it appears that both mysticetes and odontocetes evolved from a late-diverging archaeocete group known as the durodontines perhaps thirty-five million years ago, the patterns of divergence of mysticete and odontocete species and the evolutionary relationships between modern cetaceans is complex and controversial. For example, there are some who argue that sperm whales (the largest toothed whale species) are more closely related to baleen whales than to other toothed whales. There is much dissension about how current species of whales, dolphins, and porpoises emerged from the myriad webs of extinct ancestors. The issue is not easily resolved, because most of the cetacean fossil record is on the bottom of the ocean. It is further complicated by the fact that, at present, different modes of analysis have led to conflicting conclusions not easily reconciled by parsimonious explanations.

Chapter 5
MODERN WHALES

The present-day suborders of cetaceans have been developing for approximately thirty-five million years. Two general characteristics of modern-day cetaceans make them immediately distinguishable from terrestrial mammals. First, the body shape of whales and dolphins is streamlined to facilitate movement through the water. This has been accomplished through the reduction of forelimbs, the disappearance of hind limbs, the internalization of the genitals and the mammary glands, the loss of the external ear (the pinna), and development of a fusiform (tapered at each end) profile. Second, whales and dolphins have no insulating coat of hair or fur, which further enhances movement through the water by reducing the drag coefficient. In addition, the outer layer of the skin (the epidermis) is arranged in finely developed furrows called cutaneous ridges that trap a thin film of water along the surface of the body. As the animal swims through the ocean, the water trapped in these ridges moves against the external shroud of ocean water, creating an essentially frictionless interface. Further, the deeper layers of the skin (the dermis and the blubber) are rather elastic and spongelike, compensating for increased pressure on various portions of the body under higher swimming speeds.

There are approximately seventy different species of odontocetes, or toothed whales, with the number of teeth among species ranging from 1 to 260. Most of the odontocetes feed on small fish and squid, although the orca and possibly some other species like the pygmy killer whale and melon-headed whale also prey

The sperm whale is the largest of the toothed whales and dolphins, with adult males reaching a length of 60 feet.

on other marine mammals, including seals, sea lions, dolphins, and even the larger whales like the blue whale and humpback whale. Modern odontocetes are comprised of ten families, four of which are found in Hawai'i. These include Physeteridae and Kogiidae: the sperm whales; Delphinidae: the oceanic whales and dolphins; and Ziphiidae: the so-called beaked whales. The families not found in Hawai'i include Platanistidae, Pontoporiidae, Lipotidae, and Iniidae: all river dolphins; Phocaenidae: the smaller true porpoises; and Monodontidae: the beluga, or white whale, and the tusked narwhal from the Arctic.

Mysticete whales like the humpback have no teeth in the adult stage. During fetal development tooth buds form, but these never erupt. Instead they have hundreds of rigid strips called baleen hanging from the upper jaw all around the inside edge of the mouth. The word *baleen*

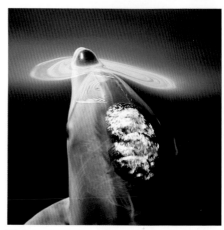

Whales and dolphins breathe through a nasal passage or "blow-hole" that is strategically situated at the top of the skull, allowing a rapid and safe exchange of air during brief surfacing episodes.

is from the Latin word for whale. The long strips of hardened material were such a diagnostic characteristic for the species that they shared the same name as the animal itself. Although the English word *whale* is related to the Norse word for whale (*hval*), both the French and Spanish words for whale (*baleine* and *ballena*, respectively) maintain the Latin connection.

Strips of baleen (called plates) are made of material similar to human fingernails. Roughly thirty to forty hairlike fibers of baleen grow out of indentations set perpendicular to the upper, outer edge of the mouth, and fuse together to form the plates. On the inside of the mouth, movement of the tongue keeps the fibrous ends of the baleen bristly and frayed—like split ends of hair, only much coarser. The frayed edges of adjacent plates of baleen intertwine, forming a filtering system that traps small fish or other marine organisms inside the whale's mouth when it lets water flow in through the front of the mouth and out through the sides. The different species of baleen whales have different lengths and widths of baleen, and different numbers of baleen plates depending on their size and their primary food source. In general, the baleen whale has between six hundred and eight hundred plates. The length of

The open mouth of a bryde's whale, seen feeding in Australia, shows that the baleen plates extending from the upper jaw are shorter toward the tip of the mouth and longer toward the back.

individual plates may range from one and a half to twelve feet, while their width may vary between three and twenty-four inches. The baleen is much shorter in the front of the mouth, and increases in length along each side, toward the back.

Baleen whales are generally separated into four families, or biological categories. These are the Balaenidae, Neobalaenidae, Balaenopteridae, and Eschrichtidae. We find that the easiest way to differentiate these families is on the basis of their feeding structures and habits.

A humpback whale pushes the tip of its head above the surface during a feeding episode. The mouth is slightly open, showing the baleen plates affixed to the top of the jaw, and demonstrating the large, bucket-shaped lower jaw.

This photo of the head of a surfacing Southern right whale shows a very narrow upper jaw, with the sides of the lower jaw reaching high toward the top of the head, and covering baleen plates twelve feet or more in length. The top of the head (called the bonnet) is covered by coarse, discolored patches of skin known as callosities.

The Balaenidae are comprised of four species—the bowhead whale, which is found only in the Northern Hemisphere; and three species of right whale: one found in the Southern Hemisphere, one in the North Atlantic, and one in the North Pacific. These whales are all characterized by their lack of dorsal fin and by a rotund figure with a large, deep mouth and a high-arching upper jaw. The "bucket mouth" whales move slowly, are found relatively close to shore, and float when dead. Consequently they were considered the "right" whales to hunt by early whalers, and were the first species to be brought perilously close to extinction. Even today the North Atlantic right whale is believed to number no more than three hundred animals, and is generally considered too far below a critical population size to avoid ultimate extinction within the next hundred years or so.

The Balaenidae feed on small shrimp-plike species called crustaceans. These include a variety of species of copepods, the most abundant multicellular animals on the planet, found in both freshwater and marine habitats; as well as amphipods and euphausiids, found in polar and temperate waters of all the world's oceans. In the Southern Hemisphere the most plentiful euphausiid, *Euphausia superba*, also known as krill, hatches and grows at an explosive rate in late spring and summer, creating huge blooms of prey on which the bucket mouth whales feed. In the Northern Hemisphere, one of the most abundant food sources in addition to euphausiids is a type of copepod known as a calanid. Tiny beasts with busy mouths and huge appetites, they are the primary consumers of phytoplankton (microscopic floating plants) in the ocean, and also feed on other co-pepods and the eggs of many fish species.

Copepods are part of the massive array of zooplankton: animals that float with the tides and currents of the ocean. Whales that feed on them have developed the skills to track ocean features (e.g., thermal, wind, tide and salinity patterns) that corral their prey. Many copepod species avoid predation by sinking far below the surface during the day, and then sneaking back up to feed at night. Whales that feed on them must adapt to such strategies when searching for food. Some of the best opportunities to watch right whales feed occurs in Cape Cod Bay (near Provincetown, Massachusetts) during the summer, where right whales can find calanid copepods in huge numbers. The whales' manner of surface feeding has been described as skimming, as they slowly swim back and forth through the swarms of tiny animals, filtering them from the vast amounts of ocean water that fills their mouths.

In the winter of 1979 we observed a lone North Pacific right whale swimming in a pod of humpback whales in Hawai'i. This was a highly unusual sighting since little was known of the abundance and distribution of right whales in the North Pacific at that time. Some believed them to be extinct. Even today it is believed there are fewer than one thousand remaining from a prewhaling estimate of eleven thousand animals. There appear to be two subpopulations: the western group in the Sea of Okhotsk north of Japan and an eastern group in the Bering Sea. We have observed southern right whales off the coast of Australia on a number of occasions.

Balaenopteridae whales are characterized by the possession of a dorsal fin (these whales are sometimes referred to as "finners" for this reason, although the name is sometimes applied strictly to the fin whale); a torpedo-shaped, relatively streamlined body; and a series of folds or pleats that run from the mouth down to the umbilicus, or navel. The pleats allow the whales to remain streamlined when swimming over long distances. When it comes time to feed, the whales are able to expand the pleats and increase their mouth size by more than three times—temporarily becoming "bucket mouths" and vastly increasing the amount of water they can engulf and filter. Because of their manner of feeding, these whales are referred to as "gulpers." When the pleated whales expand their mouths this way, one can often see areas of pink coloration between the pleats. This is due to the absence of blubber and skin pigmentation in these areas, which allows the coloration of the blood just beneath the skin to show through. Perhaps for this reason, these whales are referred to as "rorquals," based on a Norwegian whaling term that translates roughly as "red whale." A number of sources suggest that the word rorqual refers to the Norwegian term for "furrow," in reference to the pleats themselves, but this appears to be in error.

The Balaenopteridae feed on a wide range of prey, and this is reflected in differences in the number, size, and spacing of their baleen plates. Almost all of them feed primarily on krill in the Southern Hemisphere when near the Antarctic ice edge. The largest of the Balaenopteridae, the blue whale, feeds almost exclusively on euphausiids, consuming between two and four tons a day, although their diet may include amphipods and copepods in the Northern Hemisphere. The other Balaenopteridae also consume euphausiids, amphipods, and copepods, but also eat a variety of small fish species (such as sand lance, capelin, and herring), as well as squid.

With the exception of the humpback whale, rorquals look similar in body shape, although they differ greatly in size, ranging from the one-hundred-foot blue whale to the twenty-foot dwarf minke whale. Although minke whales are found all over the world, a subspecies called dwarf minke is found only in the Southern Hemisphere. We have frequently seen these while doing research in Hervey Bay

Although both belong to the family Balaenopteridae, the 90-foot blue whale (top) and the 35-foot minke whale (below) differ widely in size, habitat and behavior.

and the Whitsunday Islands in Australia. It is startling to see an animal so similar in shape to a blue whale yet barely longer than our eighteen-foot research boat. In 2006 we had a prolonged encounter with a pair of dwarf minke whales as they swam under and around our boat for nearly an hour.

The humpback is very different in looks and habit from the other rorquals. It has much longer pectoral fins, a more rotund body shape, wartlike bumps on its head, and an irregularly-shaped dorsal fin. Humpback whales are placed within a separate category, or genus, from the other six species within the Balaenopteridae family. Five species of Balaenopteridae

whales have been observed in Hawai'i: fin, sei (pronounced *say*), humpback, Bryde's (*broo'dis*), and common minke (*mink'-ee*). Neither the blue whale nor Antarctic minke have been seen here.

There is only one species in the family Eschrichtidae, the gray whale, well known for its long travels up and down the coast of California. A gray whale has never been seen in Hawai'i. Gray whale feeding patterns are distinctly different from the whales in the each of the mysticete families described above. The gray feeds largely on crustaceans that it stirs up from mud and silt on the shallow ocean floor. It therefore needs neither the bucket mouth of the slow-moving

A gray whale, shown here approaching a whalewatch boat, lacks the oversized jaws and huge head of species in either the Balaenidae or the Balaenopteridae families.

Balaenidae, nor the expandable mouth of the speedy Balaenopteridae. The gray is a streamlined whale like the rorquals, but without expandable pleats or a dorsal fin. While there are two to four short throat grooves located on the underside of the jaw, movement of these may be more important for creating suction while feeding than for significantly increasing the size of the mouth. The gray whale feeds on a variety of relatively small organisms near or on the ocean floor. One form of gray whale feeding has been described as gouging craters in the bottom sediment, then using the tongue as a piston to forcefully suck food out of the mud, through the baleen, and into the mouth.

The three general types of baleen whales described so far use widely different feeding strategies (skimming, gulping, and sucking). Nonetheless all three strategies permit individuals to feed effectively on their own. This is quite different from most of the odontocete species that usually feed in highly coordinated social aggregations.

With the exception of the sperm whale and perhaps some of the river dolphins, odontocetes tend to encircle or herd their prey as a group in order to enhance the amount of food available to each individual. These differences in feeding strategies are reflected in the nature of the social groupings formed by the different species. Odontocetes in general form much larger groups that are stable over relatively long periods of time than do the mysticetes. Groups of oceanic dolphins may number in the tens of thousands, and though one may occasionally see mysticetes in coordinated groups of more than a dozen or so whales, more often than not, they feed in groups much smaller than that.

We've seen as many as thirty-five fin whales feeding in a coordinated fashion on pelagic (open sea) red crab in the Sea of Cortez, while we circled above in a twin-engine Cessna. We have watched from our research boat groups of three to twelve humpback whales lunge-feed on small fish in Alaska, in the Gulf of Maine, and

Although baleen whales, like these humpback whales in Alaska, do not form the large groups that odontocetes do while feeding, they can sometimes be found engaging in coordinated groups of eight to twelve animals.

off the southeast coast of Australia. While some have described these episodes as cooperative, it is difficult to be certain whether individual whales are really helping each other out, or more simply taking advantage of the opportunity to exploit each other's spillover. The fact that some feeding groups maintain their associations over many years and a variety of sounds are produced by animals engaging in group feeding bouts may well support the conclusion that they are engaging in true cooperation. Whatever the relationship, it clearly does not extend to the number of animals that can frequently be seen in dolphin groups, such as the group of approximately twenty-five hundred common dolphins we once saw from the air off the coast of Mexico.

The fourth family of baleen whales, the Neobalaenidae, includes only one, little-known species called the pygmy right whale. The animal is seldom observed in the wild, although on two occasions we've seen one from our research vessel in Hervey Bay, Australia. This species is found only in the Southern Ocean. Despite its name, it seems to bear little resemblance to the right whale (it even has a dorsal fin), and adults seem not to grow longer than twenty-two feet. Neither their diet nor their feeding patterns are known with any degree of certainty.

Chapter 6

WHEN IS A WHALE NOT A WHALE?

The difference between whales, dolphins, and porpoises often generates confusion. Whales may be odontocete or mysticete (all mysticetes are whales, but not all whales are mysticetes!). All dolphins and porpoises are odontocetes. Within the suborder odontoceti, the family Delphinidae uniquely includes all three types of cetaceans—whales, dolphins, and porpoises—whereas all other odontocete and mysticete families are comprised of only one type.

In general, whales are bigger than dolphins (with some exceptions), and dolphins are bigger than porpoises (again, with some exceptions). The largest mysticete whale is the blue whale (eighty to one hundred feet), while the largest odontocete whale is the sperm whale (males grow to about sixty feet). The largest dolphins (bottlenose and Risso's dolphins), however, are larger than the smallest whales (pygmy sperm, dwarf sperm, pygmy killer, and melon-headed whales). Porpoises are

Spinner dolphins (top photo) are relatively small odontocetes, reaching seven feet as adults, while the short-finned pilot whale (bottom photo) may reach a length of 25 feet.

While not a true porpoise, the Hawaiian spinner dolphin (shown here in one of its characteristic spinning leaps above the surface) is typically called a porpoise by local fisherman.

among the smallest of odontocetes. The Gulf of California porpoise, or vaquita, for example, only grows to lengths of four to five feet, but there are dolphin species in this size range as well (Hector's and Chilean dolphins, for example).

To further complicate our understanding of the difference between a dolphin and a porpoise is the fact that there are both scientific and common uses of the terms. True porpoises are one of the species in the family Phocaenidae. These relatively small (five- to eight-foot) cetaceans are characterized by a somewhat rounded, blunt head without the dolphin's protruding rostrum, or beak. In addition, porpoise teeth are spade-shaped (like the front bottom teeth of a human), while dolphin teeth are conical. Porpoises also tend to have triangular dorsal fins, while dolphin fins are curved backwards, like the fin on the bottom of a surfboard. Nonetheless, while there is a distinct porpoise family, the use of the word has often been applied throughout history more according to local custom. In Hawai'i, for example, local fishermen commonly refer to dolphins as por-

poises. This is also true in Florida, where the term *dolphin* or *dolphin-fish* is reserved for a species of sport fish known in Hawai'i as *mahimahi* (super strong) in the Pacific and *dorado* (Spanish for "golden") in other areas. The word *porpoise* is a combination of the Latin words *porcus* (pig) and *piscis* (fish), and recognizes the relatively small but rotund body shape of species like the harbor porpoise. The word *dolphin* is a variant of *delphys*, which means "womb" in Greek.

The sub-order Odontoceti, comprised of whales, dolphins and porpoises, includes a diversity of sizes, shapes and lifestyles, such as the distinctly marked four and a half foot long Hector's dolphin, found only in New Zealand.

Chapter 7

HUMPBACKS: UP CLOSE AND PERSONAL

EXTERNAL FEATURES

The humpback whale is the fifth-largest of the great whales, and is found in all the major oceans of the world. The earliest writings that seem unambiguously to refer to humpback whales are from the mid-seventeenth century. In 1725 the British naturalist Paul Dudley provided a detailed anatomical description of the whale, based on reports from whalers working off the coast of New England. In 1756 humpbacks were first named *baleine de la Nouvelle Angleterre* (whale of New England) by the French naturalist Mathurin Jacques Brisson. Twenty-five years later, the German taxonomist Georg Borowski, employing Linnaeus's Latin binomial system, declared the humpback whale to be *Balaena novaeangliae*, but this was soon changed by French naturalist Bernard-Germaine-Étienne de Lacépède to *Balaenoptera jubarta* in recognition of the fact that the whale shared few features with other members of Balaenidae. In 1846 J. E. Gray (for whom the gray whale was given its common name) assigned the name *Megaptera longipinna*, inventing both a new genus (big wing) and a new species (long flap), thereby doubly emphasizing the long pectoral fins as a dramatic, defining characteristic of the species.

Over the next century a whole slew of species names for humpback whales found in different parts of the world were invented, based on the bumps on its head (*nodosa*), its cowlike eye (*boops*), either the size of the long pectoral fins (*longimana*) or their mobility (*versabilis*), or the location where the specimen was found (*braziliensis*). Finally in 1932 the American zoologist Remington Kellogg concluded the many different names all referred to one species, and ruled the scientific name should be *Megaptera novaeangliae*, giving precedence to Gray's genus name and the earliest designation of the species name by Borowski.

The head of a humpback whale, showing the many knobby protuberances on its head called tubercles.

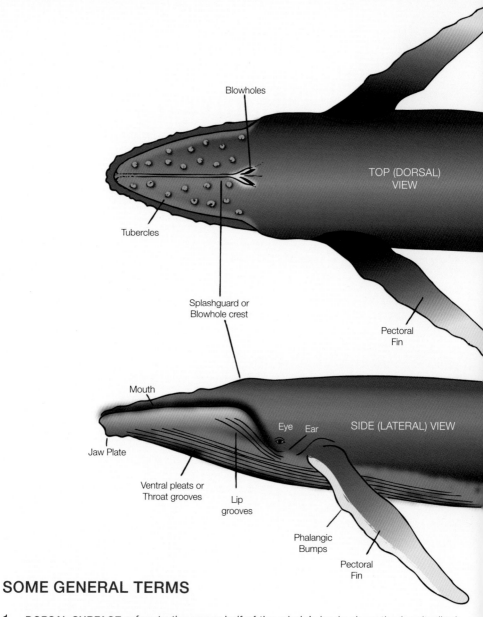

Blowholes

TOP (DORSAL) VIEW

Tubercles

Splashguard or Blowhole crest

Pectoral Fin

Mouth

Eye   Ear   SIDE (LATERAL) VIEW

Jaw Plate

Ventral pleats or Throat grooves

Lip grooves

Phalangic Bumps

Pectoral Fin

SOME GENERAL TERMS

1. **DORSAL SURFACE** refers to the upper half of the whale's body along the longitudinal axis from head to tail—that part of the whale normally seen when it surfaces to breathe, exposing the back and dorsal fin.

2. **VENTRAL SURFACE** refers to the lower half of the whale's body along the longitudinal axis from head to tail. The humpback whale's ventral grooves, umbilicus, genital and mammary slits, and anus are all located along the ventral surface.

3. **ROSTRAL ASPECT** refers to the forward extension of the whale's head, particularly from the eyes to the tip of the mouth, or rostrum.

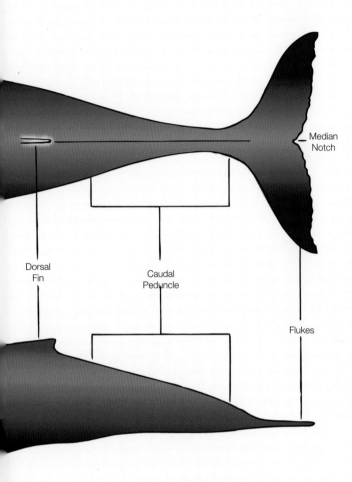

Dorsal
Fin

Caudal
Peduncle

Median
Notch

Flukes

External anatomy of humpback whale (after Bennett)

4. **CAUDAL ASPECT** refers to the rear body portion, especially the caudal peduncle, or tail stock, which extends from just behind the dorsal fin back to the tail.

5. **INVERTED** refers to the positioning of the whale when their ventral surface is uppermost. Cetaceans are normally considered right side up when their dorsal surface is uppermost. On many occasions, humpbacks engage in a number of behaviors with their ventral surface uppermost.

6. **LATERAL** refers to either the right or left side of the whale.

Like the blind men trying to describe an elephant by feeling different parts of its body, the observers of the past, focusing on the most prominent features of a dead, stranded, or harpooned whale, managed to totally miss the mark in coming up with a name. Were it up to us, after so many years of watching and listening to living humpbacks in the majesty of their own ocean home, we would recommend a name to honor unique features like their powerful acrobatic skills, the haunting song of the males, their incredible bubble displays, their facile grace underwater, or the vast expanse of ocean through which they roam.

Humpbacks display reverse sexual dimorphism in size (females are larger than males in the adult stage). North Pacific females reach average lengths of forty-five feet, and males average forty-three feet in length (sizes range from thirty-six to fifty feet). The largest recorded humpback was an eight-eight-foot female caught in the nearshore waters of Bermuda in the Caribbean. A mature humpback may weigh up to a ton per foot, or nearly forty tons when fully mature. Calves range in size from ten to sixteen feet, and average one and a half tons (three thousand pounds) at birth. In the Southern Hemisphere, humpback whales may be, on average, three to five feet longer than their Northern Hemisphere counterparts. The reason for this size difference is not known, but may be related to the fact that humpbacks tend to migrate into colder polar areas in the Southern Hemisphere than they seem to in the Northern Hemisphere. This may require a larger body mass to enhance thermoregulation (heat retention).

When viewing a humpback whale for the first time, many whalewatchers are surprised by its unusual appearance. The head of a humpback is large in proportion to its body. It comprises nearly one-third of the whale's entire body mass. The mouth line runs high along the entire length of the head, dropping sharply just before the eyes. Each eye is about the size of a large orange, and is found just above the end of the mouth line. The eyes can bulge quite significantly from the orbital cavity, allowing the animal to extend the range of its peripheral vision dramatically. During the many years we have conducted field studies on humpback whales in various

The eye of a surfacing humpback whale, showing the extent to which it can protrude from the eye socket to enhance the field of view.

settings around the Pacific, we have had frequent opportunities to be underwater with them. We have been regularly impressed by their ability to protrude their eyes to such degree as to allow them to see not only down and out to the side, but perhaps even far behind and above themselves.

The eyes are generally brown with a kidney-shaped pupil, much like the eye of an ungulate. Rarely do whalewatchers get a look at the eye of the humpback, but on occasion it does happen. In January of 2004 passengers aboard the Pacific Whale Foundation vessel *Ocean Explorer* were enthralled when a pod of three "curious" humpbacks swam back and forth under the stationary boat for almost two hours. At one point the three adults raised their heads in unison perpendicularly out of the water. They were less than twenty feet from the boat. Their rostrums (the portion of the head from just in front of the blowhole to the tip of the jaw) were five feet higher than the deck of the boat. All on board had a unique chance to look directly into the eye of not one whale, but three. Such experiences were once relatively uncommon in Hawai'i, but appear to have become more frequent over the past few years. While working in Hervey Bay, Australia, we have had many similar encounters with "friendly" humpbacks acting as if they wanted to look inside our research boat.

The ear of a humpback is located just behind and below the eye. The absence of an external ear flap makes it nearly impossible to detect the tiny half-inch ear slit. The nares, or paired blowholes, are found near the center of the head and almost midway between the eyes. An elevated area in front of the blowholes called the splashguard, or blowhole crest, prevents water from pouring into the blowholes during respiration. The splashguard, which expands when the blowholes are opened, facilitates rapid movement through the water by enabling

the animal to expose the least amount of its body above water when breathing.

The humpback's head is adorned with curious knobs, once called "stove bolts" by the Yankee whalers. These knobs, known as tubercles or sensory nodules, are each about the size of a golf ball. Although found in reduced form on other balaenopterids, they are both more numerous and more prominent on the humpback. The tubercles are distributed on the humpback's upper and lower jaws and in about the same area that facial hair is found on humans. The number and pattern of distribution of tubercles is unique to each whale. Each tubercle contains a

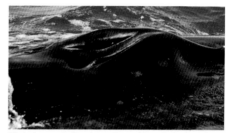

All baleen whales have two blow hole openings, while toothed whales and dolphins only have one. Humpback whales have a splashguard that rises to prevent water from going into the blow hole when the animal breathes.

Humpback whales frequently approach whalewatch boats and thrill spectators by raising their heads above the water as though trying to watch those who are watching them.

hair follicle, sometimes with a single, light gray vibrissa about a half inch to one and a half inches long. Recent research has found that each hair follicle contains nerve endings and has a well-developed blood supply. This suggests they may serve as a sensory organ, but their exact function is unknown. They may be used in courtship activity, help detect the presence of prey in "blind spots" during feeding, or aid in navigation by helping to detect current and temperature changes. The tubercles of highly active and aggressive whales (almost always males) are often seen worn raw and bleeding during the time whales are in the winter breeding grounds. The tubercles whiten after healing, which helps accent their unique spatial patterns and allows for individual identification from aerial photographs. Mothers with newborn calves are often seen nudging and carrying their calves on their heads, which may also stimulate the sensory tubercles.

Humpbacks possess a chin or jaw plate, which is an irregularly shaped shield

The tip of the humpback whale's head is adorned with tubercles, each with a single hair growing from it.

located on the midline of the lower jaw near the tip of the rostrum. The jaw plate appears to increase in size with age, and although its exact function is unknown, it has been hypothesized that males use the jaw plate as a weapon to displace other whales when fighting. The humpback's upper jaw is narrower than the lower jaw, and the tip of the rostrum is quite blunt.

The humpback whale's throat grooves, or ventral pleats, which run from the whale's chin to its navel, are deeper and fewer in number than in other rorquals. The number of pleats varies from twelve

The ventral surface of a humpback whale's head shows the barnacle-covered tubercles at the very tip, the protruding jaw plate at mid-line, and the ventral pleats extending down the length of the throat.

This photograph of the lateral and ventral surface of a humpback's head shows the unique arrangement of lip grooves just below and behind the eye, as well as the ventral grooves running along the throat area.

to thirty, with females typically possessing more pleats than males. This may enhance the female's ability to gather food in response to the increased demands of lactation and pregnancy. A series of short, curved grooves, called lip grooves, extend from the corner of the mouth to the pectoral fin, and sometimes just beyond. The lip grooves are asymmetrical, with up to six grooves found on either side of the head. Their length and position is unique to each whale, and has been used by some researchers to verify an animal's identity.

The humpback possesses a large, fleshy dorsal fin that emerges from a distinct hump about two-thirds down the back, well behind the blowholes (thus giving the whale its English common name). Dorsal fins come in a variety of shapes and sizes, and are usually not more than twelve inches in height. The exact role and function of the dorsal fin is unknown, but it probably aids the animal in maintaining horizontal and vertical integrity

in the water. Some of the great whales, such as the right, bowhead, and gray, do not possess dorsal fins, indicating that the dorsal fin may not have any more adaptive function than the earlobes of humans. The dorsal fin is comprised of connective tissue and muscle and is completely without bone. We often see the fin wobble when animals come up to blow in surface-active groups.

A little-described area of the humpback's body is the region to the rear of the dorsal fin that eventually gives way to the tail. This portion of the body is called

Each whale's dorsal fin is of a slightly different shape and size.

The tailstock, or caudal peduncle, stretches from the dorsal fin to the tail fluke.

the tailstock, or caudal peduncle. The high arching of the caudal peduncle while diving and the prominent swelling of the back ahead of the dorsal fin most likely resulted in the name "hump-backed" whale, first coined by early whalers. The dorsal surface of the peduncle sometimes has a ridged, bumpy appearance like a washboard. These bumps are sometimes referred to as the knuckles, and are protrusions of the caudal vertebrae. These become more noticeable when the animals begin to lose weight after extended periods of fasting during the winter, or perhaps when stress is placed on the skin as it expands to facilitate a pregnant mother's overall growth.

A characteristic feature that makes any whale readily identifiable is the tail fin, or flukes. A humpback's flukes are broad and flat, usually ten to fifteen feet wide, and are capable of propelling the whale at speeds of up to twenty miles per hour. The flukes are normally serrated along the trailing edge, and deeply notched in the center. Barnacles often encrust the dorsal (upper) surface and tips of the flukes, while the ventral (under) side of the flukes is characterized by a wide array of black-and-white patterns sometimes left by barnacle rings. These patterns of light and dark on

The fifteen-foot-wide tail fluke is distinctly shaped to provide maximum strength and efficiency in swimming.

The shape and coloration pattern of each tail fluke is unique to that whale.

the ventral surface are also unique to each animal, and provide an excellent opportunity to identify the same whale across extended periods of time and distance. We will discuss this further when we discuss techniques of identifying individual whales in a later section (see Chapter 14, No Two Humpbacks Look Alike).

Few whalewatchers in Hawai'i get the opportunity to view the complete ventral surface of a humpback. Some behaviors allow brief glimpses of the belly region, but typically one has to see a humpback underwater to get a better idea of what is located where. The following is a bit of a road map, working forward from the whale's tail to its head.

Just ahead of the junction of the flukes and the peduncle on the whale's underside is a protruding bump called the ventral keel, or carina (from the Latin word for keel). Although found on all whales in a variety of sizes, the exact function of the carina is unknown. It may be important for hydrodynamic balance. In some cases its size may differentiate male from female, or even one species of dolphin from another. In front of the carina lies the anal slit, through which excrement is voided into the ocean as a huge cloudy mass replete with relatively soft chunks of fecal matter. In male humpbacks there is an approximate three- to four-foot space between the anal slit and the genital slit, an opening of less than two feet, which houses the retractable penis (be patient, we'll tell you how long that is later!) The female's genital slit is smaller and much closer to the anal slit than is the case for males. Another important characteristic difference of the female genital slit is the presence of a grapefruit-size bump at the rear end of the opening. This bump, called a hemispherical lobe, can allow us to differentiate males from females, although the opportunities to view the structure seldom occur. Observers should not confuse the hemispherical lobe with the carina, which is further back towards the tail fluke.

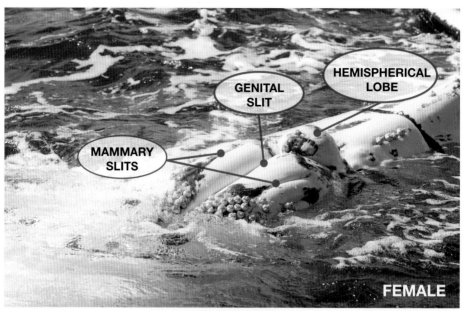

FEMALE

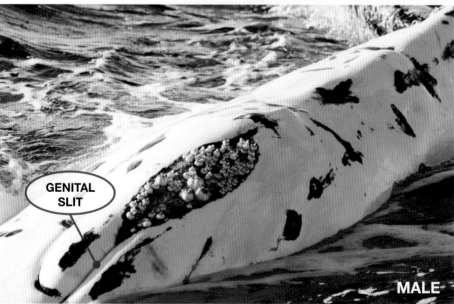

MALE

The swollen mammary glands of a lactating female (top) are on either side of the genital slit. The nipples are hidden within the slits in the mammary glands. The hemispherical lobe is shown to the rear of the genital slit. In the male (bottom photo) the genital slit is longer, further forward on the peduncle, and without a hemispherical lobe.

In both males and females there are two smaller slits on either side of the genital slit. Although little more than rudimentary grooves on males, the more pronounced slits of the females house the mammary glands and teats. Following the bodyline towards the head from the genital opening, at about the midline, is the umbilicus, or what is commonly referred to as the "belly button" (we are not certain, but we think most humpbacks are "innies" rather than "outies"). We have seldom observed a humpback calf with a portion of

It is not unusual for barnacles to attach to areas around the genital slit, as in this photograph of a female.

its umbilical cord still attached, suggesting that the cord is severed quite close to the umbilicus during birth.

Among the most striking features of a humpback are its flippers, or pectoral fins. The pectoral fins of an adult are usually about one-third or more of the body length. They are scalloped on the leading edge with an average of ten bumps protruding at the phalanges (finger bones) and joints. The shape and extension of these bumps are very important for the hydrodynamic efficiency of the whale's movement through the water. The pectoral fin is constructed to create turbulence behind the fin instead of at the fin's forward interface with the water. This minimizes the degree of "stall," or loss of lift in the animal's forward momentum, and explains in part how humpbacks can move with such incredible finesse and control.

Pectoral fin shapes vary from animal to animal: short and wide, long and narrow, or deformed (blunt at the ends, for example, or half or all of the fin missing). In 1981 we observed a male subadult who was missing his entire left pectoral fin (we nicknamed him Leftie) resting near the ocean bottom in about sixty feet of water near Mākena, Maui. The fact that Leftie was resting is not so unusual, but his method of resting was. He remained in a stationary position by balancing himself on the bottom with his rostrum and his right pectoral fin—sort of a one-handed headstand! Several days later, underwater photographer Flip Nicklin photographed Leftie off Lahaina performing his one-handed headstand once again, only this time he was singing at the same time. Besides being used as an auxiliary balancing mechanism, the pectoral fins also aid in locomotion, thermoregulation, defense, and mating. We have observed humpbacks moving slowly backward and forward by sculling with their pectoral fins. Long-distance travel, however, relies primarily on propulsion from the tail flukes.

The general body coloration of the humpback varies, but it is typically dark gray to near black dorsally, and white to light gray ventrally. The pattern of light underneath and dark on top is quite common among marine animals, and is referred to as countershading. Countershading is useful in protecting animals from their predators, and may also provide camouflage while feeding. If you peer down into the water's depths, a dark object is difficult to detect because it absorbs light and blends into its surroundings. Conversely, if you are underwater and look towards the surface, a light-colored object will reflect light and be equally hard to detect, looking much like a cloud. Whalewatchers are often surprised when they observe brilliant bands of turquoise blue near the sides of surfacing whales. This is merely the white coloration of a pectoral fin or the white scars and markings on the flank of the whale being filtered by the blue water as it reflects light back towards the surface.

Humpbacks in the North Pacific tend to be primarily dark, with a small portion of them showing limited areas of white on their bellies or pectoral fins. Humpbacks in the Southern Hemisphere, however, show a spectacular range of coloration patterns that can be grouped into one of four different marking patterns. Type-1 whales have marking along the ventral surface that extends all the way up the flanks. Type-4 animals are nearly completely dark, and Type-2 and Type-3 whales show intermediate degrees of white and dark coloration. During aerial surveys in Hawai'i over many years, we have found virtually all the whales to be of Type-1, although about 30 percent of them have extensive white markings on the upper surface of the pectoral fins. Approximately 40 percent of the east Australian whales we have studied since 1984 are Type-1 or Type-2.

In the clear waters of Australia's Whitsunday Islands, the underwater sight of whales with large areas of white along the side and across the ventral surface is re-markable. Whales with large areas of white that leap above the surface also provide spectacular displays for whalewatchers.

In Hawai'i, humpback whales are primarily dark on both the dorsal and ventral surfaces, although the pectoral fins frequently show white on either surface.

Perhaps the most stunning observation of unusual coloration in a humpback whale occurred in 1992, when we saw a completely white humpback in Hervey Bay, on the east coast of Australia. On that particular occasion the whale stayed in the bay for two days, and we successfully documented its behaviors from relatively close range in our research boat, as well as from the air. We have since documented the travels of the white whale as it has made its way up and down the east coast of Australia over the past ten years, and have published our observations, suggesting that the whale is a true albino, the only documented case of an albino humpback whale ever recorded (Moby Dick, Herman Melville's famous allegorical whale that brought down Captain Ahab, in all his pride and anger, was a sperm whale).

Migaloo, the world's only all-white humpback whale.

Following our first observations back in 1992, we got in touch with an aboriginal elder to ask what the significance of the sighting would have for indigenous people. She pointed out that albinos (whether humans or other species like kangaroos) were generally regarded as sacred. When we asked her to suggest a name, she suggested Migaloo, which loosely translates as "white fella." Although we did not know it at the time, the elder's name was well selected. A few years later Migaloo made another appearance in Hervey Bay, and a number of observers (including those on our research boat) could hear the remarkable whale singing—a certain indication that he is a male. This was later confirmed by genetic analysis in 2005. Migaloo continues to make regular appearances off the east coast of Australia and has become a famous symbol for humpback whale protection in the Southern Hemisphere. The Queensland State government has even passed special legislation preventing people from getting closer than five hundred meters to humpback whales.

Calves are light gray in color when they are newborn, darkening gradually

Migaloo is believed to be approximately 20 years old, and appears to be an otherwise normal adult male.

Newborn calves are generally lighter in color than adults.

within the first month. They frequently have milky white patches near the tip of the rostrum, around the lip area, and over the ventral surface of the flukes. We have observed small and very light calves with their mothers during aerial surveys, and a number of reports of light calves have been obtained from other researchers and boat crews in Hawai'i over the years. This supports the claim that calves are born in or near the Hawaiian islands.

Cetacean skin is highly developed to ensure insulation, sensitivity to touch, and hydrodynamic efficiency when moving through the water. The skin is well supplied with nerve endings and blood vessels, which often lend a detectable pinkish hue to the throat and belly areas, where the blubber layer is least thick. The skin consists of three layers: the epidermis (the uppermost layer, which is itself comprised of three intertwined layers), the middle layer (dermis), and the hypodermis, which consists primarily of blubber. The epidermis as mentioned earlier, is lined with shallow furrows that may aid in reducing friction between the whale and water as it swims. There are no sweat glands or hair follicles (except in a few areas around the mouth) in the cetacean epidermis, unlike marine carnivores and pinnipeds. Extensive studies of cetacean integument (skin structure) shows that the epdermis is more than 10 times thicker than in terrestrial mammals. In response to the tremendous wear between water and upper layer of the epidermis, the outermost layers of whale and dolphins skin gets renewed 10-12 times a day, compared with once a day in humans. The dermal and hypodermal layers are often infested with parasitic worms that coil up into tight balls, resulting in slight swellings or bumps. These "whale warts" may be found all over the body. They may also be the result of waterborne toxins or sun exposure.

The hypodermis replaces hair for heat retention, and is found in all cetaceans

"Whale warts" are frequently observed on cetacean skin - perhaps the result of imbedded parasites or from exposure to the sun.

in varying amounts. During the peak of feeding activity in the summer months, the blubber in humpbacks may be as thick as eighteen inches in some parts of the body. Blubber is thickest over the back and along the caudal peduncle, and is thinnest around the head and belly. Not only is the blubber important for insulation, but it is also used to store food and provide fresh water.

In Australia mothers with calves often show skin lesions behind the dorsal fin that may result from sun exposure.

Over the past few years we have documented a number of incidents in Australia in which mothers with newborn calves show lesions approximately eight to ten inches long on either side of the mid-line on the dorsal fin. This is a previously unreported phenomenon and we are concerned this may be associated with climate change. Mothers spend protracted periods of time resting at the surface with their newborns. It is possible the lesions result from high levels of ultraviolet exposure. Queensland has the highest reported incidence of human skin cancer in the world, with a high UV index resulting from the depletion in the ozone layer above the region.

During our research we have actually touched humpbacks on a number of occasions (but only at the whale's invitation!), and have found the skin soft, spongy, and surprisingly warm, feeling very much like a wet piece of neoprene. Whales have lain against our research boat

and actually draped a pectoral fin over the side of it. We have had a number of opportunities to rub the heads, pectoral fins, and sides of whales as they calmly rolled at the surface and pressed against our boat. On one occasion a large female lay upside down underneath us and gently stroked her tail fluke along the entire length of the hull, lifting us slightly up out of the water, and creating an amazing squeaking sound as her flukes rubbed against the aluminum bottom. The hull of our small boat, painted white with longitudinal furrows called strakes running from the bow to amidships, may well have looked like the belly of a calf from beneath the surface. Whatever possessed the whale to rub her flukes up against us, it was with a sense of relief when, after no more than a moment or two, we felt the boat set back down in the water and saw the whale surface to blow just ahead of us.

WHAT'S INSIDE?

The skeleton of humpback whales has evolved to accomplish a number of tasks. The skull has been reshaped to accommodate the movement of the nostrils to the top of the head; the jaws have elongated to provide a huge feeding mechanism based on a cavernous mouth and a curtain of baleen plates; the forelimbs have been restructured to essentially get rid of the arm, leaving little more than a huge shoulder, wrist, and four elongated, oversized fingers; the hind limbs have all but disappeared, leaving only vestigial (remnant) traces of internal bones; and the spine has elongated to allow the development of a powerful paddle to propel the animal through the ocean. Nature is an architect that, moving at a snail's pace, puts pragmatics ahead of aesthetics and function ahead of philosophy. Like all the species found in any given habitat at a particular moment in geologic time, the humpback whale is wondrously constructed to make its daily living in the marine environment.

Surprisingly, the humpback's skeletal system makes up only 15 percent of its total body weight. In terrestrial mammals the bones comprise more than 50 percent of the total body weight. The supportive properties of seawater help maintain the integrity of the humpback's body, ridding it of the need for heavy bones to support its weight. The bones of humpbacks are only a thin shell of compacted outer calcium covering a spongy inner network of delicate webs that surround large spaces filled with fatty marrow. The fatty marrow throughout the whale's bones accounts for nearly one-third of its body oil. This high concentration of oil even allows some humpback bones to float (approximately 80 percent of the oil content of the bones is found in the head), which in turn allows even the densest parts of the humpback's body to have a low specific gravity.

The adult humpback whale's skull is massive—approximately fifteen feet long and nearly nine feet wide. In order to house the nasal passages, which lead from the larynx (which has no vocal chords) up through the middle of the skull to the top of the head, the main area of the skull has become broadened and foreshortened. Forward of the blowholes the upper jaw arches slightly. The two mandibles (lower jaw bones), which are bowed outwards, are joined at the tips by a gelatinous material. Buried in the back of the massive head, the humpback's brain weighs between twelve and sixteen pounds (a human brain weighs three pounds; a bottlenose dolphin's brain, five pounds; an elephant's, eleven pounds; and a sperm whale's brain weighs twenty pounds—the largest brain of any known animal). The blue whale has a brain about the same size as a humpback's, even though a blue whale's total body weight is probably three times that of a humpback.

Humpbacks possess fifty-three vertebrae: seven cervical (neck), fourteen thoracic (chest), ten lumbar (pelvic area), and twenty-two caudal (tail area). Humans have thirty-three vertebrae. Interestingly, we have the same number of neck vertebrae (seven) and almost the same number of thoracic vertebrae (twelve). The biggest difference is in the number of lumbar (we only have five) and caudal vertebrae (called sacral and coccygeal vertebrae in humans, which only total nine compared to the whale's twenty-two). Clearly cetaceans have devoted a lot of their spinal structure to ensuring a powerful tailstock. Like all cetaceans, humpbacks have specialized bony attachments on the underside of the caudal vertebrae called chevron bones, not found on terrestrial mammals. Chevron bones provide for increased muscle attachment to aid in powering the flukes while swimming. Humpbacks also have the first and second cervical vertebrae (the atlas and axis) fused together, minimizing

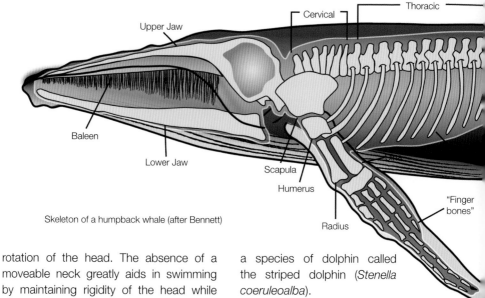

Upper Jaw

Cervical

Thoracic

Baleen

Lower Jaw

Scapula

Humerus

"Finger bones"

Radius

Skeleton of a humpback whale (after Bennett)

rotation of the head. The absence of a moveable neck greatly aids in swimming by maintaining rigidity of the head while moving at higher speeds. The thoracic and lumbar vertebrae have a high percentage of cartilage allowing for greater elasticity and flexibility of body movement while swimming.

The flukes of a humpback are not modified hind limbs, but are in fact a combination of muscle, blubber, and ligament over a heavy fibrous tissue, extending over and beyond the coccyx, or tailbone. There are no bones in the flukes proper. The loss of the hind limbs has been accompanied by reduction of the pelvis to a small slender bone that is unattached to the vertebral column. This small remnant of the hind limbs, called the vestigial bone, is perhaps the last lingering link the humpback has with its terrestrial ancestors. Occasionally cetaceans are observed sporting hind limbs. Whaling records dated 1949 from Vancouver Island, Canada, report a harpooned humpback with eighteen-inch, nonfunctional hind limbs protruding from its body wall. Scientists aboard Japanese whaling ships in the 1950s and 1960s reported finding pelvic bones in minke whales and hind limbs protruding from sperm whales and

a species of dolphin called the striped dolphin (*Stenella coeruleoalba*).

The pectoral fins are modified forelimbs complete with many of the bones that are present in our own arms and hands. The forelimb has become flattened and paddle shaped by foreshortening of the upper arm (humerus), as if the elbow is attached directly to the scapula, the large, flat shoulder blade that supports extensive muscle attachments. The bones of the lower arm (ulna and radius) are short and thick. Nearly half of the fifteen-foot-long pectoral fin consists of the carpals, metacarpals, and phalanges (hand and finger bones). Rorquals have four "fingers," while the other mysticetes and the odontocetes have five.

Humpbacks possess teeth only during the early stages of fetal development when a series of vestigial teeth form. The upper jaw hosts twenty-eight small, blunt, conical teeth on each side, while forty-two teeth can be found on either side of the lower jaw. The teeth are resorbed and disappear before birth. Baleen plates are present prior to birth, measuring about one to two inches in length. There are about 300 pairs of baleen plates found inside a humpback's mouth. The actual number in

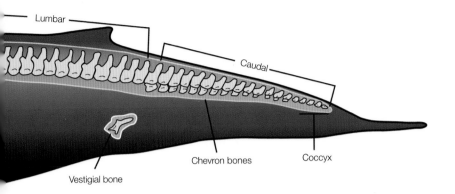

Lumbar

Caudal

Chevron bones

Coccyx

Vestigial bone

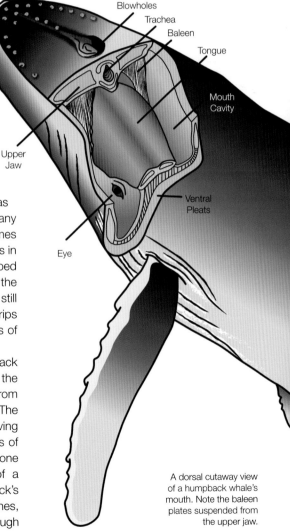

Blowholes

Trachea

Baleen

Tongue

Upper Jaw

Mouth Cavity

Ventral Pleats

Eye

A dorsal cutaway view of a humpback whale's mouth. Note the baleen plates suspended from the upper jaw.

any given humpback may range from 270 to 330. Humpback baleen is deep gray or black with lighter, near-yellow end bristles. The maximum length of humpback baleen is two and a half feet, with an average width of ten inches. There are thirty-five to forty bristles per plate.

Whalers used to refer to baleen as "whalebone" and valued it for making many products. It was used to form the frames of hoopskirts and umbrellas; as stiffeners in women's corsets; and as webbing in bed frames, chairs, and carriage seats. In the far north, where bowhead whales are still hunted, the Inuit split the baleen into strips and weave them into wickerlike baskets of incredible durability and strength.

The tongue of an adult humpback weighs about two tons. Although the tongue is movable, it cannot protrude from the mouth as it can in other mammals. The tongue is instrumental in feeding by moving food to the esophagus. The esophagus of a humpback is much narrower than one would expect, about the diameter of a large grapefruit. Although the humpback's throat could expand to about ten inches, this wouldn't have been quite wide enough to swallow Jonah.

A surfacing whale, its lower jaw extended, and water pouring through the baleen plates, obtains a mouthful of schooling prey. Note the blow of a second whale to the left, probably catching what the first whale may have missed.

The mouth cavity of a humpback becomes enlarged during feeding through the movement of the lower jaw and the expansion of the ventral pleats. The bottom jaw can open to approximately 90°, creating a gape nearly fifteen feet in height, and a mouth like a front-end loader capable of holding twenty tons of water (approximately five thousand gallons— enough to fill a twelve-by-ten-foot backyard swimming pool to a depth of seven feet). The lower jaw is controlled by a complex system of well-developed muscles unique to the rorquals, rather than the relatively simple attachments of ligament found in other mammals. This suspension system permits the incredible gape achieved during feeding, and provides a cushioning mechanism against the stress of sudden entry of vast volumes of water. Water and prey are drawn into the mouth not only by the whale's forward momentum, but also by the expansion of the ventral pleats and the sudden backward motion of the tongue. The powerful set of muscle attachments to the lower jaw (called the frontalmandibular stay) and the elasticity of

the ventral pleats allows the whale to snap its mouth shut rather quickly, trapping its prey inside. The pleats are then drawn tight, and with the help of the massive tongue, water is driven out of the mouth through the baleen plates, which filter out the food items. These are then forced back into the esophagus by the tongue.

The esophagus gives way to the stomach, which is comprised of three main compartments: the fore stomach, main stomach, and pyloric stomach. This probably reflects the phylogenetic connections with terrestrial ruminants such as cows, deer, and camels. Food passes from these specialized stomachs to the intestines, which are about five times the body length, or nearly two hundred feet long.

While we have seen the humpback's huge mouth in operation a number of times while watching them feed in Alaska, off the New England coast, and even during their southward migration in Australia, those episodes always involved observations above the water's surface. Because the areas where whales feed usually have so much nutrients and prey in them, it is not very easy to get a good look at them below the surface. On one occasion in Hawai'i, however, we had the rare opportunity to see an adult humpback underwater as it dropped the lower jaw until it was nearly perpendicular to its body, and then slowly close it while the pleats expanded, tripling the dimensions of its normal girth. The animal then partially opened its mouth twice, swimming slowly by, directly ahead, perhaps thirty meters away. As it closed its mouth the second time, the ventral pleats could be seen to undulate as water was expelled from the mouth and the throat returned to its normal size. The whale swam across our path as it trailed a group of about ten animals, including a calf, which had disappeared only moments before. Since it was clear the whale was not feeding (there were no schools of fish in view), we concluded it may have been a low-level threat display, and quickly returned to the research boat. We have also witnessed humpbacks in Hervey Bay open their mouths during

heavy rainstorms. Local fishermen claim the whales are getting a drink of sweet, fresh water or rinsing their baleen.

The respiratory apparatus of the humpback whale is designed to facilitate rapid recharging of the lungs while minimizing the time spent at the surface. The blowholes lead to a short, stout trachea, which can measure nearly a foot in diameter. The connection from the nares (blowholes) to the trachea is much more direct in whales than in terrestrial mammals. A unique system of valves prevents air from entering the mouth during exhalation, and water from entering the trachea during inhalation. Although there is no direct connection from the trachea to the mouth cavity, it appears it is possible for a humpback to slightly dislodge its trachea enough to exhale air into the mouth. While it is unclear whether or not humpbacks have a functional olfactory capability (sense of smell), there are three nasal cavities located in the cartilage below the blowholes that are lined with

The blow of a humpback rises approximately eight to ten feet above the head, and shows the exhalations from the two blow holes combining to form a pear-shaped cloud of expelled moisture.

olfactory epithelium, which is a cellular layer generally invaded by nerve fibers that connect to the olfactory bulb. Although toothed whales and dolphins do not have an olfactory bulb (the end of the long, thin extension of the olfactory nerve, which is nested in the very base of the brain), the mysticete whales do, although it is poorly developed.

Located in the barrel-shaped thoracic cavity, the lungs are relatively light but still long enough to fill a Cadillac stretch-limousine. In humpbacks the lungs account for less than 1 percent of the body weight, compared to 7 percent of overall body weight in humans. It has been reported that the lungs of cetaceans are asymmetrical in size and shape, with the right lung usually larger and longer, probably to accommodate the huge heart.

The thorax and abdomen of a humpback are very rigid, with a long, powerful ligament running just below the spinal column to ensure that the spine does not sag. There are fourteen pairs of ribs. The humpback's rib cage is not capped with a sternum, as is the case with terrestrial mammals. Instead a single

bone joins just the first two ribs, allowing the remainder of the free-floating rib cage to flex and accommodate increased pressures from deep dives. Consequently one of the most serious problems that a beached humpback faces is the crushing of the lungs due to displacement of the ribs as the extraordinary weight of the body bears down on the rib cage.

Whale hearts, as one might guess, are huge. The largest of all belongs to the blue whale. It weighs about 1,500 pounds (think VW Beetle), and it is frequently said that kids could play in the aorta. A humpback's heart weighs about 450 pounds. Because of the dorsal position of the lungs and the barrel shape of the thorax, the heart of the humpback has become much more elongated than that of most terrestrial mammals. The whale heart is responsible for pumping up to two or three times more blood per unit of body weight than in humans. An adult human contains just under a gallon of blood. Perhaps as much as 750 gallons (weighing three tons) of blood flows through the veins of a whale the size of a humpback. That amount is equivalent to the amount of household

Although a humpback whale can stay submerged for more than 30 minutes, its lungs account for less than one percent of its body weight.

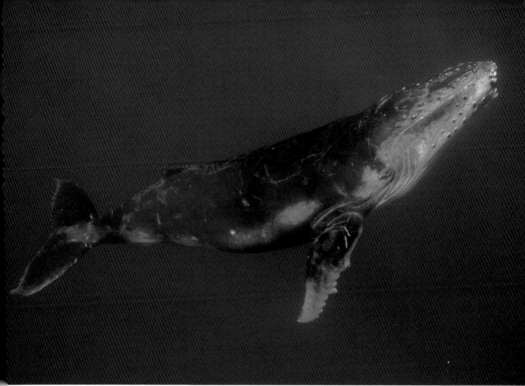

Three hundred feet below the surface, the humpback whales heart beats only three to five times per minute.

water an average American uses in one week.

Because of the size and power of the humpback's heart, scientists have been intrigued by whether it is any more advanced or efficient than that of terrestrial mammals. The vascular system has been modified to meet the demands of the pressures of the deep. Startlingly large veins, up to four inches in diameter, are found in the vertebral canal. The heartbeat of a whale is much less frequent than that of a human. Physiologists suggest there is generally an inverse relationship between heart size and heartbeat. Monitoring a whale's heartbeat is no easy task! Ideally, one would want to monitor it both at the surface and as they dive, since it has been established that diving mammals slow their heartbeat considerably to conserve oxygen and deal with the problems caused by anaerobic (without air) conditions. They can't really be kept in captivity, and even if they could, it would be difficult to determine how stress might effect the heartbeat. Stranded whales have had their heartbeat taken, but again this only provides information about highly stressed animals. Using the highly sophisticated underwater listening devices on submarines, scientists have reported eavesdropping on the heartbeat of free-ranging large whales, including the humpback. At the surface, the powerful heart of the humpback beats only six to ten times per minute, and drops to half of that by the time they have dived to one hundred meters. It has recently been suggested that tiny cellular structures known as nanowires allow the humpback whale to send critical electric signals through large masses of blubber to maintain the rhythmic, coordinated beating of the huge organ. These nanowires may someday be used instead of costly pacemakers in humans, reducing the cost and removing the need for surgery.

One major adaptation of marine mammals has been the development of a spongelike aggregation of convoluted blood vessels called the rete mirabile (literally, the marvelous network). In cetaceans the retia mirabilia (plural) are found around the heart and lungs, in the sinus cavities of the head, and in areas of the pectoral fins and tail flukes. These networks help conserve body heat and enhance oxygen storage. Surrounded by spongy tissue, they may also serve as shock absorbers during deep diving.

Humpbacks have an enhanced oxygen-carrying capacity because they have a high blood volume, high levels of red blood cells in their blood, and each of the red blood cells is heavily loaded with hemoglobin (an oxygen-binding molecule in the blood). Compared with humans, whales also have high levels of myoglobin (an oxygen-binding molecule in muscle cells), providing an enhanced ability to function during breath-hold dives.

Humpbacks have the continued problem of dehydration while living amidst a sea of salt water. They extract their fresh water from the prey on which they feed, or from their blubber reserves during periods of fasting such as the winter breeding season. The salinity of a whale's blood and other bodily fluids is higher than that of terrestrial mammals, but is still much lower than that of seawater. Consequently, humpbacks are in danger of either absorbing too much salt from the ocean, or losing too much fresh water. To maintain proper salt balance, whales have to pass large quantities of highly concentrated urine and limit all other water losses. Water loss is inhibited in part through an efficient respiratory system (which limits the amount of moisture lost while breathing), the absence of sweat glands, and by a high metabolic rate.

The kidneys of humpbacks are specialized for increased concentration of salt in the urine. They are long, flat, broad organs divided into as many as three thousand lobes. This large number of lobes (cattle have only twenty-five) helps remove salt from the bloodstream, and provides for more concentrated urine production. The feces of humpbacks also permit additional discharge of salt from the body.

Little is known about how much or how often humpbacks excrete feces or urine, particularly while fasting during the winter, although in recent years researchers have been trying to collect fecal samples to determine the relative occurrence of various prey items in the whale's diet. We have witnessed whales defecating numerous times: We once observed a newborn calf let out thin, mustard yellow strips about eighteen inches long and two

The mustard-colored discoloration in the center of this photograph gives evidence that a whale just defecated.

HUMPBACKS: UP CLOSE AND PERSONAL

A gray whale, lying on its back, waves both a killer-whale scarred pectoral fin (left) and the tip of his eight-foot-long penis.

inches wide, which floated for nearly two minutes and then began to dissipate in the water. On another occasion we were following a large adult near Kahoʻolawe to obtain a photograph of its tail flukes when it suddenly dived, and as it flicked its tail fairly high into the air, an eruption of yellowy brown, very watery fecal material burst from its anal region. We tried not to take it as a personal comment. A third event involved a stranded whale in Australia that defecated twice while it was lying helplessly in wet sand some two hours before we were able to finally get it back into the ocean. Near Eden, Australia, where we see humpbacks feeding, we also frequently observe them defecating. While the food may have been fresh, the odor emitted wasn't!

The reproductive organs of humpbacks are located internally, enhancing the body's streamlining. The penis of an adult male is approximately four to six feet long and eight to ten inches wide at the base. Its testicles weigh around forty-five pounds each at their maximum size during the mating season. While these figures may suggest rather enormous reproductive equipment, the organs of the humpback are actually on the small side for the large baleen whales. A fifty-foot right whale in full reproductive readiness may be expected to have an eight-foot-long penis, and testicles that weigh an amazing one thousand pounds each! Erection of the penis is accomplished by a pair of muscles attached to the base, as in cattle and horses. As the muscles relax, the penis emerges from the genital slit, and an erection is supplemented by a sudden influx of blood. Erections in humans and carnivorous mammals are accomplished primarily through an influx of blood. When the muscles attached to the whale's penis are retracted, the penis is drawn back inside the genital slit, and it takes on an S-shape to better fit into the cavity. The testicles are located behind and lateral to the kidneys and above the penis. They are long, cylindrical organs that increase in size as increased sperm production takes place. Although sperm are present all year, an increased amount of semen develops in the winter months.

The female's ovaries are found in the same relative location as the testicles of males. The ovaries of immature females are smooth and flat, but in the adult they resemble a bunch of grapes, weighing as much as fourteen pounds. Within each grape, or follicle, is a minute spot known as the ovum, or egg. When the follicle matures, it ruptures, discharging the egg into the fallopian tubes, a process known as ovulation. At this time the female is ready to mate. Although rare, it is possible for two follicles to ripen and simultaneously discharge two eggs into the fallopian tubes, potentially resulting in twin fetuses should successful mating occur. Since twin calves have never been observed in Hawai'i, however, it must be assumed that only one fetus reaches term.

Once the egg is released, the follicle begins to increase in size, forming new tissue which is pink in rorquals but yellow or gray in all other mammals. The follicle at this stage is known as the corpus luteum of ovulation. If the egg is not fertilized, the corpus luteum begins to degenerate within twenty days of ovulation, and the pink tissue disappears, leaving a white-tissued body called the corpus albicans. If the egg is fertilized, the corpus luteum begins producing progestin, a hormone that stimulates and strengthens adhesion of the egg to the uterine wall. The corpus luteum continues to function throughout pregnancy, but begins to resorb after the calf is born, until only a corpus albicans remains. In humpbacks, the corpora albicantia never disappear completely, which helps scientists to evaluate the frequency of ovulation. Unfortunately, there is no indication from corpora albicantia as to whether or not a pregnancy occurred.

Humpback whales usually ovulate once during a winter breeding season, although whaling records indicate two or even three ovulations may occur within the same season. Ovulation during the summer would be expected rarely, if ever, although incidents have apparently been documented. If a female becomes pregnant in a given year, the calf will be born the next winter, following a ten- to–thirteen-month gestation period. Although postpartum ovulation (ovulation immediately after giving birth) has been documented in the ovaries of females killed by commercial whalers, it is an exceedingly rare event. Consequently, it is believed that a normal, healthy female will give birth every two years at the peak of her reproductive ability.

The calf is born in Hawai'i following a 10- to 13-month gestation period.

Vision has limited utility in the light-depleted world underwater, making it imperative that whales have a well-developed auditory system.

MAKING SENSE OF THE SENSES

Our knowledge of the humpback's sensory capabilities is based on what has been learned from studies of smaller cetaceans maintained in laboratory settings, and inferences from field observations. In addition, descriptions of the visual system have resulted from examination of specimens recovered during whaling operations, and physiological analysis of stranded and beached specimens.

The general picture that emerges from these various observations and investigations is that humpbacks have superb vestibular (balance) control, keen tactile sensitivity, excellent hearing, good vision, a sense of taste in at least some areas, and rudimentary (if any) olfactory capability.

In order for a highly mobile species to survive, it is imperative that mechanisms exist for both short-range and long-distance interrogation of the environment. Because the density of water is approximately eight hundred times greater than that of air, and it is filled with particulate matter, light

penetration underwater is considerably reduced over distances of more than a few feet. The filtering and light scattering effects of seawater blur, occlude, and discolor objects seen below. Irregularities at the water's surface due to waves and wind create all sorts of changes in available light, and distort apparent distance. Even variations in cloud cover and the need for animals to operate at different depths for a variety of reasons place incredible demands on the mammalian visual system. Water is not a friendly medium for the gathering of visual information.

On the other hand, sound transmission is much enhanced underwater. The denser medium allows sound to travel five to six times faster in water than in air and, at some frequencies, farther than in air. Differences in temperature layers can create sound channels that direct energy across long distances. Consequently, the auditory system is a better candidate than the visual system for transmitting or receiving information over long distances. It should come as no surprise, therefore, that cetaceans have a very highly developed sense of hearing. This is reflected both in the adaptations within the ear itself, and in the elaborate development of the auditory processing centers within the brain.

Localization of sound sources in mammals depends upon the ears receiving separate signals that differ slightly in terms of intensity and time of arrival. While these differences are slight, they are critical. A sound that reaches both ears exactly simultaneously with equivalent intensity cannot be readily localized. For terrestrial mammals the sound receptors are little hairs that are isolated in fluid-filled containers (the cochlea) in an air chamber deep within the bony structure of the skull. The receptors are connected to the outside world through the moveable bones of the middle ear (the ossicles, comprised of the hammer, anvil, and stirrup), attached to the eardrum on one side and a thin membrane on the cochlea (the oval window) on the other side. Although relatively strong vibrations in direct contact with the bones of the jaw and head can generate the perception of sound, we normally hear airborne sounds as a result of vibrations in air, acting on the eardrum, and transferred by the ossicles through the fluid in the cochlea to the receptors of the inner ear.

The size of the head, and therefore the distance between the outer ears, has evolved in each species as a precise correlate of how fast speed travels in air. Off-center sounds must travel farther to reach one ear than the other, and the brain has specialized areas to track these differences in time of arrival, which allows us to localize sound (determine its location in space). Since the density of biological tissue is equivalent to that of seawater, however, sound can travel through bone and tissue much more easily underwater than in air. In addition, because sound travels much faster in water than in air, the terrestrial brain's ability to track temporal differences in the arrival of sound to the two ears is lost when underwater.

Whales and dolphins have overcome this problem by the development of retia mirabilia, the blood and foam-filled structures of the sinus cavities that surround the middle and inner ears, creating an air barrier that helps restore localization ability. These air "cushions" also protect the ear from damage due to radical changes in pressure during deep dives. In addition, the structure that encases the middle and inner ears of many animals (called the auditory bulla) is much more heavily developed in cetaceans as a complete bony structure, which is suspended by ligament and muscle, thereby reducing the effect of vibrations traveling through the skull. The ability to detect and differentiate changes in the

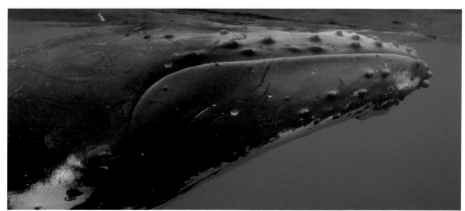

The size of the humpback whale's head, the absence of external ear flaps, and the similar density of salt water and biological tissue create significant challenges for the mammalian auditory system underwater.

Because the ear flap has been lost during evolution in order to improve hydrodynamic efficiency, the location of the ear is observable only as slight indentation directly behind the eye, about one third of the distance to the pectoral fin.

frequency (pitch) of sound traveling through water requires that sounds be produced at amplitudes (intensities) that are some four times greater than would be necessary in air. Consequently the structures of the middle ear of marine mammals must be much heavier and more rigid than those of terrestrial mammals in order to protect the delicate receptors in the inner ear.

Additional modifications have occurred with the outer ear to enhance hydrodynamic streamlining, and to prevent water from being forced under pressure against the middle ear structures. Unlike most terrestrial mammals, cetaceans have no external pinna, or earflap. Mysticetes also have a heavy wax plug that grows within the auditory meatus (ear canal) to keep water out.

There exists a great deal of controversy about the exact nature of the mechanisms involved in cetacean hearing, especially with regard to the role the external ear plays in relaying sound to the inner ear through the bony structures of the middle ear. Two opposing theories have generally been put forth. On the one hand, a number of researchers have argued that the external ear is relatively unimportant in sound transmission. Instead, they propose that sound pressure changes are "telegraphed" through the bones of the lower jaw, which contain fatty deposits that connect to the bulla of the middle ear. A more recent version of this model based on simulated sound sources activated in the skull of a dead Cuvier's beaked whale suggests the sounds actually enter the head between the jaws through the throat and then to the bony ear structures. Other researchers argue that the ear canal is as functional in marine mammals as in terrestrial mammals. The resolution of the issue is difficult, as it is nearly impossible to carry out neuroanatomical studies on living animals under the best of conditions, and totally impractical to consider doing so on an animal the size of a humpback whale. Current information supports the position that in odontocetes the lower jaw or throat is the primary channel for sound

While only useful at relatively short distances underwater, the humpback whale eye appears highly developed and capable of functioning both underwater and above the surface.

conduction, while the ear canal may be more important for mysticetes.

Regardless of the specific channel through which the sounds are received, it is clear from field observations that hearing is an important sense for humpback whales. It would be impractical to conclude that a species would have the capability to produce the elaborate vocalizations that can be heard from humpbacks without a similarly elaborate hearing system. In addition, it is apparent that humpbacks are aware of the presence of other whales and boats at considerable distances. It is extremely difficult for a swimmer to approach a whale without alerting the whale. On one occasion, we approached a calf that had strayed from its mother. According to our shore-spotters, the mother was nearly a half mile away. On our approach the calf made two or three jaw-clapping noises, which resulted in an immediate and high-speed approach by the mother, who then physically moved the calf some distance away. Clearly there is need for concern that ever-increasing noise generated by recreational boat traffic and commercial shipping in the vicinity of breeding humpback whales may interfere with their social organization and mating activities. It has already been shown that North Atlantic right whales have changed their calls in compensation for increased background noise caused by ship traffic. While it has been found that short-term

changes in duration of humpback whale song have resulted from human-generated noise, further work needs to be done to determine the possibility of long-term changes in other song attributes.

There is a rather widespread misconception that whales and dolphins have poor eyesight. This mistaken notion is based on the expectation that an eye developed on land will be useless underwater and the assumption that vision is so restricted underwater as to be pretty much useless in any case. In fact, it appears that most species of cetaceans have quite good visual ability both underwater and in air. The cetacean eye has developed a number of modifications to handle changes in available light with varying depths and to protect the eye from direct contact with the ocean and the particulate matter therein, from the high salt content of seawater, from the different demands of focusing in aerial and underwater vision, and from the pressure ranges experienced in deep diving.

The thickness and rigidity of the humpback's sclera, or skin of the eye, allows it to maintain its shape under increased atmospheric pressure. The eye is surrounded by a shock-absorbing system of rete mirabile. The eye of a humpback whale, like that of other cetaceans (with the exception of the Ganges River dolphin) has a fish-eye (nearly circular) lens that allows light to focus properly on the retina

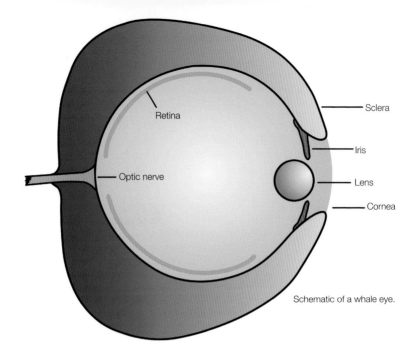

Schematic of a whale eye.

Labels: Retina, Optic nerve, Sclera, Iris, Lens, Cornea

underwater. Such a lens is ill suited for focusing light rays in air, and there is no evidence that cetaceans have the muscle attachments to change the shape of the lens in order to focus on objects at varying distances in air. But this problem has apparently been overcome, in part, by the development of an irregularly shaped cornea that acts like a bifocal lens, which compensates for the inability of the fish-eye to properly focus light on the retina in air. Consequently, when a cetacean looks at something in air, it appears to be rolling its eye back in its socket as it attempts to view through the flattened portion of the cornea. In addition, the retina is covered with a special highly reflective material called the tapetum lucidum (literally, "bright tapestry"), the same material that causes the eyes of cats and other nocturnal animals to appear to glow at night. This reflective material enhances the eye's ability to gather light and improves vision under conditions of low illumination, such as would be found with increasing depths beneath the water's surface.

Cetaceans have no true tear glands, but specialized glands around the eye (Harderian glands) produce a transparent mucous that continuously bathes the eye. The substance is believed to protect the eye from contact with salt water and the material in it, and may even reduce friction between the eye and the ocean. It has also been hypothesized (but never established) that in air, the mucous may serve to aid in focusing.

Because the whale's eyes are situated one on either side of its huge head, it would appear that the visual fields of the individual eyes do not overlap. This is not the case, however. While the predominant visual field of the whale is outward to either side, there is an area below the whale's head and forward of its eyes that can be viewed stereoscopically (with both eyes). This otherwise small area is enlarged by the mobility of the whale's eyes within the sockets. By bulging the eyes out a few inches, the overlap in the visual field is increased. Like rabbits, humpback whales appear also to see somewhat behind themselves, if the object of interest is far enough out from the midline of the body.

The cetacean eye appears to be specialized for brightness and motion detection. It does not contain color receptors, so as far as we know the humpback is color-blind, with its most sensitive light-detection capability in the blue range of the spectrum. Nonetheless, vision serves as an important sense in gathering information at close range. The wide variations in brightness patterns among whales facilitate individual visual identification, and the extraordinary range of visual displays humpback whales employ make it clear that visual communication is an important feature of their behavior. It may also be the case that aerial vision plays a role in migration. Changes in daylight or the movement of celestial bodies may guide the whale over deep ocean distances, while prominent landmarks may facilitate orientation near shore.

Considerable interest has been developing over the last two or three years in the issue of whether or not cetaceans might derive information for location and movement from differences in the magnetic field of the earth's crust. This has been studied most often in the odontocetes, and some intriguing results have been found. There is evidence that areas where dolphins are most frequently found stranded are characterized by high levels of magnetic noise or anomalies. Little work has yet been done with baleen whales, and it remains questionable whether or not humpback whales detect differences in magnetic fields.

The humpback appears to have a well-developed tactile sense. There are a number of body areas that are highly sensitive, including the lips, genital area, sensory nodules, and areas of the pectoral fins. The importance of tactile stimulation is especially apparent when watching the interactions between mother and calf, and the activities of whales in apparent courtship maneuvers.

While there is little evidence that cetaceans have the ability to smell, it has been established that at least some species of odontocetes discriminate a variety of tastes. While such experiments have never been conducted on humpback whales, it is quite probable that chemoreception (chemical reception, e.g., through taste buds) plays a role in feeding. The distribution of a variety of baleen species in their feeding areas can be predicted on the basis of salinity patterns in the ocean associated with accumulations of zooplankton and other food resources. Taste may play an important part in communicating hormonal and emotional states in the odontocetes, who may be frequently observed swimming through the trails of fecal material often excreted in social groupings; whether any of the baleen whales have sufficient development of the taste buds to permit the same patterns of use is not known.

Humpback whales have an exquisite sense of balance and body orientation. While they often appear clumsy and ungainly as they surface to blow, when viewed underwater they can be seen using their pectoral fins and tail flukes to move easily and quickly in any direction, turning at a moment's notice to their side or back. Such movement in mammals is largely controlled by an area of the brain known as the cerebellum, a convoluted structure attached to the base of the rear surface of the brain, at the top of the spinal cord. The cetacean brain is remarkable for the relatively large size of the cerebellum, compared to those of other mammals.

The humpback whale is well adapted to extract a wide range of sensory messages from its watery world, as well as from the air above it. Humpbacks have a complex and well-tuned sensory processing system that allows them to both perceive and learn from their environment and each other.

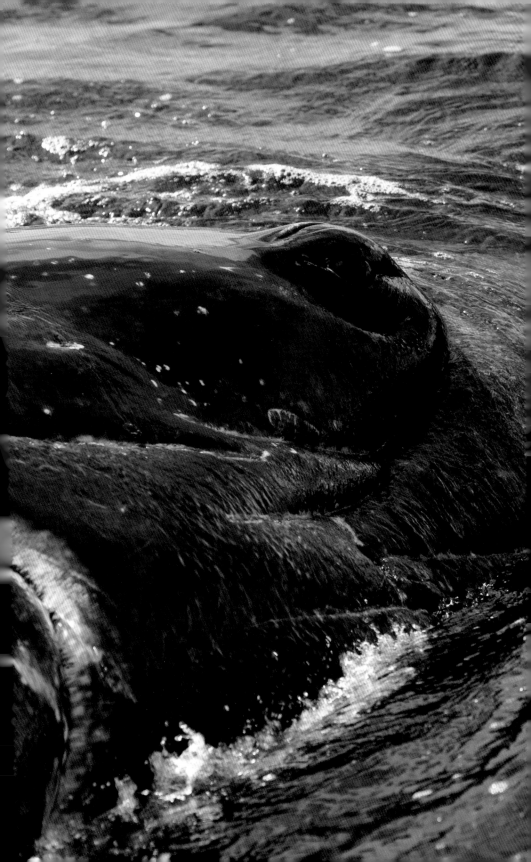

Chapter 8

MEETING THE CHALLENGES OF A WATERY WORLD

BREATHING

A whale is usually first detected by the sight of its blow, the by-product of exhalation. When a whale inhales, it fills up its lungs to capacity each time and then exhales 90 percent of its air supply with each breath. Humans exhale only 25 percent of their lung capacity. The humpback's exhalation takes a mere half second, with air escaping the blowholes at over two hundred miles per hour; inhalation takes place in a leisurely second.

Since humpbacks breathe through their blowholes, the connections between the trachea and the mouth are extremely limited. The separation of air and food passageways safeguards the animals from having water forced into their lungs when feeding. The blowholes have nasal plugs that remain closed until forced open by respiratory contractions. Since breathing is a voluntary act with whales, the opening of the blowholes is a measured and calculated event. Humans on the other hand breathe reflexively, in response to increased carbon dioxide in the blood.

Humpbacks often make a variety of airborne sounds during respiration, sometimes resembling trumpets, horns, and flatulence. These sounds may result from deformations of the nares (the blowholes), or they may be the result of controlled fluctuations in the movement of the nasal plugs. The sounds may have important social significance. The humpback blow is characteristically a tall, pear-shaped, single spout. There is some individual difference in the blows of different

animals, however, and we have observed a wide variety of types, including a double or V-shaped blow most often characteristic of a right whale spout.

How the blow of a humpback is formed is debatable. It has been suggested that the blow results from the air in the lungs being under great pressure. When expelled quickly, air from the lungs cools as it comes into contact with the outside air, resulting in condensation that produces a vapor. While this may explain some of

The blow of a humpback whale is a forceful exhalation of air in a compressed period of time that results in a tell-tale cloud of water that rises high above the whale's head.

the blows created in Alaskan waters, it seems unlikely that such would be the case in the warm Hawaiian breeding grounds. Because of the cool air, the vapor from a humpback blow in Alaskan waters will remain suspended above the water for several minutes, while in Hawai'i blow vapors are seldom observed for longer than thirty seconds.

The blow of a humpback is probably formed by a combination of water near the blowholes and moisture and mucous found within the respiratory tract. Humpbacks are occasionally observed allowing small amounts of water into the open blowholes after exhalation. This water is more than likely a natural part of the respiratory process, similar to the residual water that is ever-present in the bottom of a skin diver's snorkel. When the animal exhales, this water is quickly atomized and sent skywards in a twenty-foot-high plume.

Any whalewatcher downwind of a humpback when it surfaces will note that the blow is water-saturated, resulting in saltwater spray on the clothing and camera lens. Since all whales can transmit viral diseases through their respirations, one should never inhale the blow. On some occasions the blow of whales smells like four-month-old fish. It turns out that whales with stinky breath may be infected with a form of whale "flu." In Australia, scientists are trying to determine if the vapor from the blow may have chemical or other hormonal implications of reproductive status. As a rule of thumb: if a whale blows nearby, hold your breath—and your nose.

The blow of each whale forms a unique shape, depending upon the individual animal and the nature of its activity.

The flukes and the pectoral fins provide humpbacks the ability to move through the water with exquisite finesse.

SWIMMING

A humpback swims by moving its flukes up and down rather than from side to side like fish. Steering is accomplished by the use of the laterally placed pectoral fins and by bending of the body. The dorsal fin may also aid in stability, similar to a sailboat's keel. For many years it was suggested that cetaceans swim by beating their flukes in a corkscrew manner. In the early 1960s, however, the actual method of locomotion was established through the use of motion pictures. Forward propulsion is achieved by a forceful downstroke aided by the powerful muscles connected to the chevron bones of the caudal vertebrae, while the upward stroke serves only to reposition the flukes.

The ability of whales to move through the water depends on more than movement of the flukes. Buoyancy adjustments through movement of air within the body allow resting or stationary whales to exercise considerable control while surfacing. In addition to steering, the pectoral fins may be used to move the body both forward and backward.

Humpbacks are not fast swimmers; while able to achieve speeds of up to twenty miles per hour for short periods of time, they average three to eight miles per hour during migration. The orca can move at a maximum speed of some twenty to thirty miles per hour. The speed at which humpbacks move is highly dependent upon their activity. For example, humpbacks feeding in Alaska travel slower

Although humpbacks can swim at a high speed for short distances, they average three to eight miles per hour during migration.

than they do in Hawai'i during the breeding season. It might also be that water temperature and body weight have some effect on speed of movement. Although it may be expected that mothers and calves would move along at a rather sedentary pace, we have actually observed them swimming at speeds of ten to fifteen miles per hour when being pursued by males. There are a number of ways in which the calf keeps pace with the mother. Calves typically swim just above the mother's pectoral fin and to one side of her dorsal fin. This may allow the calf to benefit from the slipstream created by the mother. We also have observed mothers actually supporting calves on their pectoral fins or back as they swim along.

Humpbacks often leave a smooth, slick area on the water's surface after slipping under (see photo below). This was once believed to result from oily deposits washed off the whale's skin as it dove. It seems clear, especially after aerial observations of diving whales, that the slick results from vortices created through water displaced with each beat of the flukes.

Often a series of such slicks, referred to as the whale's footprints, or *puka* (the Hawaiian word for "hole"), can be seen. This allows researchers and whalewatchers alike to detect where a whale has just submerged.

Underwater, the whales often seem to glide by without moving a muscle. One beat of the flukes has sufficient power to move a whale over a considerable distance. The coordinated movement of fin and fluke is keenly developed, despite the impression of early whalers that humpbacks were ungainly and cumbersome. During our underwater

The beat of the whale's tail just below the surface creates a distinct vortex called a footprint, or *puka*.

encounters with humpbacks we have been impressed with their ability to exercise precise control over their movements and position. Many times we have found ourselves on an apparent collision course with a curious whale. With a slight roll of the body and a tilt of the flukes, the whales easily avoid us.

DIVING

Humpback whales spend the major portion of their life within six hundred feet of the surface. On the summer feeding grounds, their food source is relatively near the surface so they need not dive deeply. Although they do not feed in Hawai'i, they spend most of their time within the one-hundred-fathom (six-hundred-foot) contour. Recent observations using underwater cameras and depth recorders show that humpbacks do dive as deeply as nine hundred feet and often remain for an extended period at or near the bottom. Humpbacks do not suffer from compressed-air diseases such as the bends, which can kill scuba divers, since they do not breathe compressed air when diving. Because of this they avoid the diver's problem of nitrogen from previously inhaled compressed air expanding at the surface. When the humpback dives, its lungs are compressed so that air is forced into the nasal passages, windpipe, air sacs around the lungs, and around the sinuses in the head. This also prevents the absorption of harmful nitrogen through the lung wall. The blood, which contains a high amount of oxygen storage particles called hemoglobin, stores 40 percent of the whale's oxygen.

Although adult humpbacks can stay submerged for as long as sixty minutes, they usually stay down for no more than ten to fifteen minutes. Calves surface more often, generally every three to five minutes. Three or four breaths at the surface are usually sufficient to replace the spent oxygen. Stressed humpbacks, after being chased by other whales or boats, will often blow rapidly a number of times as though panting. This allows them to supercharge their bodies with oxygen before diving deeply for a prolonged period.

Whales must maintain an internal temperature that may be more than twice as high as the temperature of the ocean they swim in.

THERMOREGULATION

Humpbacks maintain a body temperature between 97°F and 99°F while contending with surface water temperatures that vary from 42°F in Alaska during the summer to 72°F in Hawai'i during the winter. Since water conducts heat nearly thirty times faster than does air, swimming humpbacks must regulate their body temperature under high heat-loss conditions. They do this in several ways. Because they have a low body-surface-to-internal-volume ratio, they are able to conserve heat efficiently. Relative to the whale's massive internal bulk, it has little "coastline" exposed to the water because of its fusiform shape and minimal external appendages. This permits more heat to be generated by the relatively extensive internal structure than is lost through the body wall. In addition, the thick blubber

layer of a humpback serves, in part, to reduce heat loss. Though most of the whale's blubber reserves function as food storage and fuel for migration, a small portion of the blubber is necessary for insulation.

Besides having a heat-conserving body shape, humpbacks are able to alter their metabolic rate to adjust to extensive temperature changes. Generally, because

Seasonal changes in blubber thickness may help the whale thermoregulate.

of their thick blubber, large whales maintain a lower basal metabolism rate (amount of heat generated at rest) than smaller cetaceans. In extreme low-temperature conditions, however, or when the blubber thickness becomes much reduced during the winter months in Hawai'i, the metabolic rate can be raised sufficiently to keep body temperature within its critical boundaries.

Body heat is also controlled through a complex mechanism known as the countercurrent circulatory system, first described by Norwegian physiologist P. F. Scholander. The circulatory system is arranged so that at the extremities, the arteries carrying warm blood from the heart spiral around veins carrying cool blood back to the heart. The exchange of heat between the two systems serves to ensure that the heat lost from warm arterial blood passes to the venous blood rather than through the skin into seawater. This system may be bypassed when the whale is overheated, permitting heat loss into the ocean.

The countercurrent circulatory system helps ensure that warm blood flowing from the heart heats cool blood returning from the extremities.

The three layers of skin (the outer epidermis, middle dermis, and inner hypodermis, or blubber) have little circulatory connection with each other. This ensures minimal heat loss through the body surface. Finally, decreased respiration rates also decrease the amount of warmth lost while breathing.

Shark bites expose the complex construction of whale skin - showing the high proportion of body covering devoted to blubber.

Resting whales may sometimes lie just below the water's surface, making them particularly susceptible to ship strikes.

SLEEP

Humpbacks can often be observed hovering just below the surface of the water, eyes closed, lying motionless save for an occasional movement of a pectoral fin or fluke. Females with calves will often rest at the surface with just the blowholes exposed (sometimes causing sunburn to the back and dorsal fin and often resulting in a host of reports of stranding by concerned whalewatchers).

Whale sleep is different than the sleep experienced by humans. A resting humpback appears to place itself in a sleep rhythm. Every fifteen minutes or so it will slowly rise to the surface, blow, and then resubmerge. Whales rely on a string of such "naps," rather than engaging in an extended period of sleep as humans do.

Unlike terrestrial mammals, cetaceans cannot seclude themselves during periods of sleep. They still face risks from predators, and the demands of thermoregulation and respiration remain. Cetaceans appear to have adapted to sleeping in an ocean environment by developing sleep stages that allow the continuation of important physiological processes and monitoring of the environment. Laboratory studies of dolphins suggest that during sleep the two cerebral hemispheres are able to engage in different levels of brain-wave activity. That is, one hemisphere may essentially be in a state of rest while the other hemisphere remains alert. In addition there appears to be an absence of REM sleep, the period of sleep associated with dreaming in terrestrial mammals. The differential activity level of the two hemispheres during sleep in dolphins is referred to as "unihemispheric slow-wave sleep." Research has also

A mother resting at the surface in shallow water cradles her newborn calf beneath her pectoral fin. Mothers often stay in relatively shallow water, close to shore, perhaps to avoid deep water predators or large pods of males competing for access to sexually active females.

suggested developmental differences between dolphin sleep patterns and human sleep patterns. Newborn humans typically spend up to 80 percent in one stage of sleep or another, and the need for sleep appears to diminish with age. Newborn dolphins and orcas are almost continuously active and longer periods of sleep develop with age.

Recently we have observed a number of single whales and mothers with calves exhibiting a prolonged behavior known as "tail rise," or "fluke extension." Hypotheses about this curious behavior run the gamut from thermoregulation, to a nursing posture, to a whale going for a bit of a "tail sail" (not unlike a sailboarder). Our experience has been that these whales appear to simply have fallen asleep. They have dropped into a deep snooze with their heads pointed to the ocean floor and their tails to the surface, and as they sleep they slowly pop up like corks with the flukes exposed above the water. We have spent many hours next to these "tail-rising" whales and found they are in such a deep slumber they fail to even recognize our presence!

Chapter 9

HOW SMART IS A WHALE?

We are frequently asked how "intelligent" whales are. Unfortunately, there is no direct answer to the question. The concept of intelligence is vague. Even with reference to the human species there is little agreement on what is meant by the term. We prefer to ask how well a species is able to adapt to the changing demands of a volatile environment. In this sense, an intelligent species is one that decides what to do

in the present on the basis of a complex integration of information derived in large part from past experience. Ideally, the past experiences that influence present decisions include not only what

a given individual has experienced, but also what conspecifics (members of the same species) have experienced. Viewed in this way it can be seen that intelligence is dependent upon complex learning capabilities, abstract information processing skills, and an intricate social communication network. The challenge is to figure out how to measure these capabilities in a forty-ton animal. Fortunately, there are solutions to the problem other than trying to find a way to keep a humpback whale in a testing tank long enough to give it an IQ test.

There are at least three lines of evidence to suggest that humpback whales do engage in complex mental processes. The first has to do with the amount of brain matter whales have for learning and information processing. Harry Jerison, a professor of comparative neuroanatomy (the study of the brain structure of different species) at UCLA, has developed a method for ranking species in terms of their "thinking" power. The method is based on the assumption that, for any given body size, a minimum brain size is required in order to make that body function properly. As an analogy, one might consider that the air conditioning unit required to keep a one-bedroom condominium cool is not going to be sufficient to keep a fifty-story

While observing whales in their natural environment, one often realizes that the observer becomes the observed.

office building cool. One can, theoretically at least, take an average of the brain sizes of the different species that have a similar overall size. This should suggest the size of brain it takes to run a body that size. It can be assumed that any individual species that has a brain bigger than average for its body size has extra brainpower available for thinking and problem solving. The amount of brain mass exceeding what's needed for the basic functioning of a body that size can be used to compute an index of intelligence called the encephalization quotient, or EQ.

When the encephalization quotients for a wide range of species are compared, Jerison finds that humans, primates, and cetaceans rank highest in the amount of brain material available for intellectual functioning. On that basis, we might expect to find that humpback whales show a wide range of learning capabilities. There is some

disagreement as to whether relationships between body size and brain weight tell us much about intelligence. One thing that must be considered is that baleen whales are not subject to the same constraints on body size that may limit growth in terrestrial mammals and predatory odontocetes. This might invalidate comparisons of brain-to-body-weight measures between terrestrial mammals and baleen whales.

A second line of evidence indicating intelligence in humpback whales concerns the actual structure of the cetacean brain. Not only is the brain of the humpback whale large, it is structurally complex. Most notably, the humpback, like other cetaceans, has a richly elaborated cerebral cortex. The cortex is the outer covering of the brain, where it is believed much of the activity associated with thinking and problem solving occurs. Although the cetacean cortex is somewhat thinner than the cortex of humans and nonhuman primates, it appears to be somewhat more convoluted (folded). The general impression is that the structural complexity of the cetacean brain is quite capable of supporting abstract information processing and integration skills.

Recent studies of the neuroanatomical structure of cetacean brains have shown that humpback whales have cortical structures that in some ways differ significantly from primate and human brains, while nonetheless sharing critical features associated with the development of complex social patterns. For example, the architecture of cortical layers in the humpback brain retains ancient features that are not apparent in primate brains. This suggests that the horizontal communication among neurons occurs more predominately in primate brains while the most effective patterns in humpback brains are vertical. At the same time, the discovery in humpbacks of what are known as spindle neurons—otherwise found only in the higher primates—suggests important similarities in ways the brains work. It has been suggested that the development of these similarities are adaptations that enable highly developed social abilities including sophisticated communication skills, formation of intricate bonds between individuals, and the ability to transmit new learning to offspring. What is interesting about these capabilities is that they appear to have emerged independently in cetaceans and higher primates over about fifteen million years. That is, even though primates and cetaceans are not related evolutionarily, they have converged in the development of neurophysiological adaptations to ensure somewhat similar patterns of complex social networking.

The third line of evidence suggesting that humpback whales are capable of complex mental processes has to do with their communication skills. We discuss elsewhere aspects of the humpback whale's communication system (see page 113). Rather than duplicate that discussion

Although most of their life occurs beneath the ocean, humpbacks are acutely aware of life above the surface as well.

The complexity of social behavior observed in whales suggests high levels of cognitive capability.

here, we will simply note that there is a great deal of evidence that humpback whales have the ability to signal each other for a variety of purposes. As is true of so many other aspects of cetacean behavior, we know very little of the specific meaning of the many sounds heard. Inroads are being made, however. Analyses of right whale sounds recorded off Argentina have shown that some intriguing relationships exist between the sounds made within groups of whales and the activities in which they are engaged. It is hoped that efforts to understand the sounds of humpback whales will be met with similar success. Attempts are currently under way to understand the meaning of a variety of social sounds emitted by humpback whales.

There seems little doubt, overall, that humpback whales are intelligent, according to our earlier definition. The feeling is strongly supported by observations of humpback whales in the field. It is very important that, as scientists, we avoid slipping into anthropomorphizing and fantasizing about the levels of "thought" and "emotions" that may be present in the whales we observe. Nonetheless, we cannot avoid developing a deep attraction for these awesome beings as we watch them traveling along Hawai'i's tropical shores looking for mates, caring for their young, learning about the responsibilities and opportunities of a maturing humpback whale, and competing vigorously for the opportunity to pass their genetic heritage on to the next generation. And, all the while the whales are here, the plaintive cry of their song seems to reach out and challenge us to work that much harder to understand the complexities of their life

Chapter 10
FINDING FOOD

Whales are a part of a relatively short food chain, which begins with phytoplankton that floats in the upper layer of the sea. Phytoplankton synthesizes sunlight into energy and in turn is consumed by zooplankton. The zooplankton and phytoplankton are the food source for small fishes, and together these links in the chain are consumed in large quantities by the whales. The chain is completed when waste products from digestion and dead whales sink to the floor of the ocean and decompose. This decomposing matter, also known as detritus, is recycled as nutrients for the phytoplankton.

Humpback whales have yet to be observed feeding in Hawai'i. They appear to primarily feed during the summer months in the food-rich waters of southeast Alaska and the colder polar waters further north. Their diet is a mix of euphausiids (krill), copepods, and small fish, primarily herring and capelin.

Humpback whales are filter feeders, straining their food from the water by means of baleen plates. As described earlier (see page 31), baleen whales are divided into three filter-feeder types: skimmers, gulpers, and suckers. Skimming whales (for example, right and bowhead whales) move along slowly at the surface with their mouths wide open, through blooms of zooplankton; gulpers such as rorquals (including the humpback) take in large quantities of food by rushing at it from the side or below; and suckers like gray whales create suction with the tongue and palate to draw water and food into the mouth.

Baleen plates help humpback whales strain their food from the water.

The fringed interior of the humpback's baleen plates forms a fibrous mat suspended from the roof of the mouth. The whale opens its mouth to engulf a large

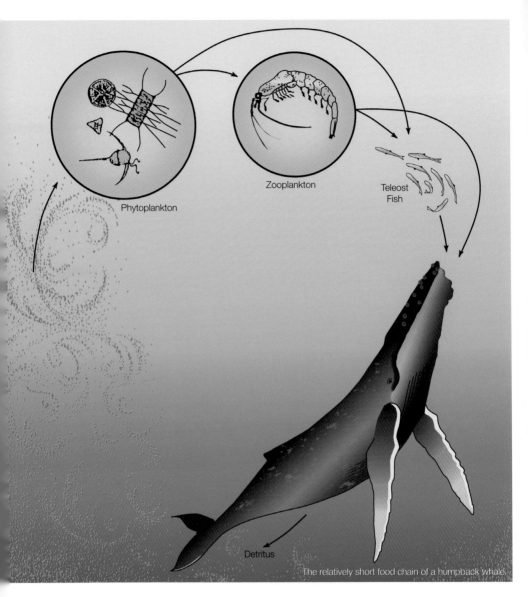

Phytoplankton

Zooplankton

Teleost Fish

Detritus

The relatively short food chain of a humpback whale.

quantity of water. The animal then pushes its tongue upwards and drives the water through the spaces between the plates. When the food becomes trapped within the fibrous mat, the whale draws its tongue posteriorly, carrying the food mass toward the rear of the mouth cavity to the throat and esophagus.

Humpback whales, like other rorquals, employ a style of feeding known as lunge feeding. This contrasts significantly with the style of feeding exhibited by right and

Humpback whales are referred to as lunge feeders.

Expansion of the ventral pleats ensures maximum advantage during lunge feeding.

bowhead whales called continuous-ram feeding. Humpbacks employ a variety of lunge-feeding techniques related to the species and density of the prey. Lunge feeding appears to be used when krill, herring, or capelin are abundant. When lunge feeding, the humpback swims rapidly through an aggregation of its prey, opens its mouth near the surface of the water, and engulfs the prey. Lunge feeding may occur in any of three varieties: vertical, lateral, or inverted, depending upon the orientation of the animal in respect to the surface.

North Pacific humpbacks use a specialized vertical lunge feeding technique known as "bubble netting." During bubble-net feeding the whale locates an aggregation of prey, dives below, and discharges a line of bubbles from its blowholes while turning in a broad arc. As the bubbles ascend, they form a noisy, visible ring, or "net," which appears to disorient the prey. The whale apparently swims towards the surface while releasing the bubbles, blocking the fish on the sides,

The unique structure of the humpback whale jaw allows the mouth to open 90°.

and pushing them up with its body. At the surface the bubbles appear as discrete basketball-size spheres. As the spheres join to form a ring, the fish coalesce into a tight ball within the closing net while the whale rises from below, bursting through the surface with its mouth open, engulfing the concentrated fish.

If the fish is herring, hundreds of them may often be observed leaping into the air. Seabirds frequently dive-bomb the whales in order to capture the leaping fish. They are not always fast enough to avoid being swallowed themselves. Thoughts like these ran through our mind early one July afternoon in Alaska as we sat in a ten-foot inflatable boat waiting for a group of feeding whales to surface. With a sound like percolating coffee, bubbles began to appear just off one side of our boat. We showed little concern until we began to realize that we were in the middle of the forty-foot net and not beside it! As the net continued to close, a mad scramble ensued for the oars. We had just enough time to realize we didn't have oars when the bubble net ceased. The whales apparently decided they didn't like the taste of researchers, for they soon surfaced through another net thirty yards away.

North Pacific humpbacks primarily feed on small schooling fishes, and do so at a pretty leisurely pace. Their South Pacific counterparts, however, frequently feed on fast-moving Australian krill (*Nyctiphanes australis*) that move at speeds of thirty miles per hour. About three hundred miles south of Sydney, Australia, is a beautiful area known as Twofold Bay off the town of Eden. Here, since 1996, we have had the amazing opportunity to watch South Pacific humpbacks feeding in the months of September and October during the Southern Hemisphere migration back to the Antarctic feeding grounds.

Humpbacks will often feed together in coordinated groups.

Bear in mind that this area is more than one thousand miles from the recognized feeding grounds of Antarctica. Never have we observed whales feeding so intensely and steadfastly, bringing a whole new meaning to the term "lunge feeding." They break the surface every twenty to thirty seconds in a continuous and riotous attempt to swallow as many of these fast-moving, orange crustaceans as possible. This type of lunge feeding frequently occurs in concert with two or more companion whales, also known as echelon feeding. It appears that for the whales of Eden, the more the merrier when it comes to corralling their tiny prey.

Once at the surface, the whale snaps its mouth shut, ensnaring its otherwise fleet prey of schooling fish.

Whales feeding in Alaska during the highly productive summer months.

A humpback can consume nearly a ton of food in a day's time. Whales feed opportunistically during the summer feeding period, engorging themselves when large concentrations of prey are found, and fasting between periods of plenty. These alternations between feeding and fasting mirror the annual cycle of a general period of summer feeding activity followed by an extended period of fasting during the winter breeding season. Humpbacks are well suited to this strategy of traveling long distances between areas of plentiful food and areas of favorable temperature. Their blubber constitutes both a natural pantry and superb insulation against the cold.

The evolution of lunge feeding involved highly specialized adaptations to both the mouth area and the tail. The lunge-feeding rorquals create incredible opposing forces known as "drag" when they stretch their ventral pleats and engulf quantities of fish and water that may actually be greater than their own body volume. Incredible power is required in the tail to move the body to the surface, and unique jaw structures must be used to keep the lower jaw from ripping away from the body as a result of the weight of the water and prey. The specialization of the jaw that developed resulted in an ability called mandibular kinesis, which essentially allows the lower jaw to unhinge during maximum extension. This capability freed the rorquals from limitations in feeding and therefore limitations in size. Rorquals like the blue whale consequently became the largest creatures to inhabit the earth.

Chapter 11

ENEMIES

Man is the only known terrestrial predator to threaten humpback whales. In the ocean whales are known to face two natural predators: sharks and orcas (*Orcinus orca*). In recent years there is growing evidence that calves in particular may be threatened by false killer (*Pseudorca crassidens*), pygmy killer (*Feresa attenuata*), and melon-headed whales (*Peponocephala electra*).

Sharks typically attack sick, distressed, or injured animals. In Hawai'i large, pelagic (open ocean) sharks like the tiger, hammerhead, and the Pacific gray have been documented feeding on whale carcasses. There have been a number of occurrences of tiger sharks attacking live humpback whale calves over the past thirty years. One can assume many more attacks go unwitnessed by humans.

In 1975 a newborn calf appeared in Molokini crater off the southern end of Maui without its mother. It was physically emaciated, as though it had not been fed for some time. The mother had either died or had abandoned her calf. After several days in Molokini, the calf became very weak. Soon an increasing number of sharks began to invade the crater. A large, ten-foot tiger shark made an initial pass at the calf. When the weakened calf showed little ambition to defend itself, the shark tore off half of its left pectoral fin. In less

A voracious tiger shark rips huge bites of blubber and skin from a wounded humpback whale.

A hungry orca beaches itself in successful pursuit of a South American sea lion that failed to move as quickly as the terrified remainder of the group.

than twenty minutes Molokini crater was a pool of blood and the near-two-and-a-half-ton calf was consumed.

In the winter of 1994 we observed a tiger shark feeding on a dead, stranded calf in the nearshore surf a short distance from our research offices. Two years later a whale that had been entangled in fishing gear and released nonetheless stranded on a reef offshore in Kīhei and was attacked and killed by tiger sharks while we watched. This was clearly a case in which sharks took advantage of a dying animal, but that may not always be the case. In March of 2002 we received a report of a solitary humpback whale calf swimming erratically about one hundred yards offshore. We contacted the National Marine Fisheries Service (the federal authorities that monitor marine mammals). Before they arrived however witnesses saw a tiger shark attacking the pectoral fin and tail flukes. Within two hours the dead calf was pulled below the surface by multiple tiger sharks, and it was not seen again.

The orca, also known as killer whale, is typically thought to be the only cetacean to feed on other warm-blooded species, including pinnipeds (seals, sea lions, fur seals, and walruses) and other cetaceans. Attacks by captive pygmy killer whales on other small odontocetes in captivity, however, have also been documented. It has also been reported that pygmy killer whales attack humpback whales in the wild. There is evidence that closely related species such as the false killer whale and melon-headed whale also attack humpbacks. Although a number of pinniped species have been observed feeding on the carcasses of other pinnipeds, the orca is the primary marine mammal known to hunt, attack, kill, and consume other marine mammals.

It is now well known that orcas attack humpback whales. These attacks appear to take place more often in colder waters than in warmer waters, consistent with the distribution patterns of orcas. There exists some debate among scientists about the extent of predation by orcas and whether it is more opportunistic or a common occurrence that might influence recovery

The missing section of the left side of this whale's tail may signal a close encounter with a shark or orca.

from whaling. Pacific Whale Foundation researcher Patricia Naessig examined the scar patterns on the tail flukes of more than 3,400 humpbacks we identified in Australia from 1984 to 1996. She reported approximately 17 percent of the animals showed evidence of orca attack. There is little evidence that animals showed additional scarring across successive sightings, indicating that most predation occurs on calves and juveniles. Some researchers have argued that migration, in large part, may be motivated by the need to avoid high levels of predation in the summer feeding areas. A more recent worldwide analysis of orca predation indicates that attacks on humpback whales are a relatively infrequent and opportunistic occurrence.

Prior to the 1990s sightings of orcas in Hawai'i were considered rare, and there were no humpback attacks documented. Since then the number of orca sightings have grown dramatically. In 1995 we were sent surface and underwater photographs of a group of five orcas, including one male, observed by a boat captain off the coast of Kaua'i. The following year we heard of sightings near the island of Lāna'i. In 1997 we were told of another sighting of five animals near Maui, and a lone orca was reported off the coast of O'ahu. In March

of 2000 a group of five orcas was reported near Ni'ihau, west of Kaua'i Island. Later that year, we observed a group of six orcas west of Lāna'i in September. In 2001 a boat operator sent us photographs of orcas with humpback whales near Kaua'i, and reported that he and his passengers

The spacing of the scars, and evidence of fresh wounds on this whale's tail suggest a recent attack by an orca.

had watched them feeding on one of the whales. In 2004 a female orca stranded on the island of Lāna'i, while a second was observed off shore. The cause of the death and stranding is still not known. A recent report by Robin Baird and his colleagues also describes a number of orca sightings off the west coast of Hawai'i Island between 1993 and 2003, including attacks on humpback whales and spotted dolphins. Analysis of available photographs

Male orcas can be supremely skilled hunters of other marine mammals, working alone or in packs of up to one dozen animals.

The scars and open wound on this humpback whale calf, abandoned by its mother, resulted from repeated attacks of a tiger shark.

showing dorsal fin identifications reveals that these are not the same animals being observed repeatedly, and shows that there is a growing number of orcas inhabiting Hawai'i for at least part of the year.

In Australia our research team observed orcas in the vicinity of feeding humpback whales near Eden, off the southeast coast, during two days in mid-November of 1998. On the third day reports were received from fishermen that orcas had been seen attacking a calf. By the time our research boat was on site, all that could be found were large pieces of flesh floating at the surface. We once observed five orcas attack and feed on a number of bottlenose dolphins off the Queensland coast of Australia. Orcas have also been reported near our study site in Hervey Bay. Additionally our researchers in Ecuador report regular occurrences of orca sightings. Overall, the patterns of orca observations that we have described indicate a high correlation in tropical waters between the presence of migratory humpbacks and the increased presence of orcas.

Groups of orcas form a diverse and complex social system, including extended family groups that inhabit well-defined nearshore areas and looser aggregations of animals that range far into deeper water. The long-term stable groups of orcas found near shore feed primarily on fish. The less well-known offshore animals are more likely to feed on other marine mammals. Hunting in coordinated groups, the marine mammal eaters render their victim defenseless by removing portions of the flippers and flukes. Feeding usually involves tearing long strips of flesh from the helpless whale. Whalers claimed that orcas prefer the tongues of the great whales, and reported they forced open the mouth of a dead whale to tear out its tongue.

Humpbacks are not defenseless against such attacks. According to the Australian scientist Graham Chittleborough, humpbacks in Australia use their massive tail flukes as a weapon, thrashing out at the attacker. Humpbacks have been observed in Hawai'i breaching and tail slapping in the vicinity of sharks and may do the same when attacked by orcas. Humpbacks can use their huge, elongated skulls to ram a threatening opponent. They can affiliate with other nearby whales, or attempt to out-swim or out-dive predators. Adult humpbacks have some refuge in size but the small calves are more vulnerable.

Chapter 12
IRRITANTS

The various knobs, folds, bumps, and creases of a humpback's body play host to a variety of parasites. The most numerous and obvious external parasite (ectoparasite) is the barnacle. Barnacles come in a variety of sizes, shapes, and colors, and can attach themselves directly to the skin, to other established barnacles, or can embed themselves in the flesh. The barnacles do not actually feed off the whale, but use the whale as a base, allowing them a better opportunity to feed on planktonic marine organisms as they hitchhike across the ocean. They may be considered parasitic because the weight and profile of large aggregations may interfere significantly with the whale's hydrodynamic capability. Humpbacks have been found with as much as one thousand pounds of acorn barnacles attached to them! The barnacles most often associated with humpbacks are the acorn barnacles (*Coronula diaderma* and *C. reginae*). They can be found attached to the flukes, flippers, head, and tubercles. Acorn barnacles flourish in the polar waters and then drop off in the warm waters of Hawai'i, often leaving a white ring of scar tissue. Acorn barnacles seem to be attracted to humpbacks because of their

Whales play host to a variety of barnacle species, which can attach to many parts of the body.

Humpback whales have their own unique form of louse, *Cyamus boopis*.

relatively slow swimming speeds.

Other barnacle species, such as the gooseneck barnacle (*Pollicipes polymerus*) and the rabbit-ear barnacle (*Conchoderma auritum*), are not as adept as the acorn barnacle at attaching to the whale's skin. They must rely on anchoring on established barnacles, and well-sheltered spots such as the ventral grooves and genital slit. These barnacles also flourish in the feeding grounds and drop off by the time their host has reached the warmer breeding grounds.

Near the base of the barnacles live small, pale, spidery parasitic animals that feed on the humpback's skin. These tiny crustaceans are whale lice, or cyamids, belonging to the family Cyamidae. The cyamids are not free-living. They survive only on whales, like many other species-specific lice. The humpback's unique species of whale lice, *Cyamus boopis*, is about one inch long with strong claws attached to each of its ten legs. Other

crustaceans, small copepods sometimes referred to as water fleas, can be found living on the humpback's baleen plates among the end bristles and burrowed deeply into the whale's flesh.

It appears that when a whale becomes immobilized by sickness or injury, whale lice proliferate. In 1996 we encountered an injured humpback just off the coast of

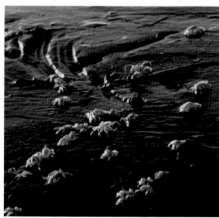

When whales become ill, they soon become infested by whale lice that feed on their skin.

This whale was so encrusted with orange whale lice we nicknamed him Rusty.

Maui that was so encrusted with orange whale lice that we nicknamed him Rusty. Underwater examination showed that he had a severely deformed caudal peduncle that may have resulted from a ship strike.

This photo of a whale tail from Western Australia shows the characteristic patina of color associated with a covering of diatoms.

We also noticed five large tiger sharks and decided it was time to get back in the boat. As night fell, the sharks moved in . . . two days later we found the remains of his partially devoured carcass.

Another incident in 1996 gave us a firsthand opportunity to experience what pests whale lice can be. An adult humpback whale died just off Kīhei on the south end of Maui. Its death appeared to

be the result of entanglement in fishing gear that it had dragged all the way from Alaska. At low tide we began taking vital measurements and attempted to remove the gear. Any physical contact with the whale's body led to an immediate attack of biting, nipping whale lice. They were impossible to ignore and difficult to dislodge. One can only imagine the pain such an infestation must create on the highly sensitive skin of a humpback whale.

Microscopic organisms, such as algae and diatoms (especially various species of the genus *Cocconeis*), flourish and bloom on the humpback's skin. Quite often whales observed in Alaska and new arrivals to Hawai'i have a yellowish green tint to the lighter portions of their bodies. This tint effect is caused by green algae, and is striking to see on whales with all-white tail flukes and pectoral fins. In the Southern Hemisphere we have seen whales from the Antarctic with a more orange hue, caused by a particular species of *Cocconeis* known only in the southern polar regions. A whale observed by our research team in Ecuador earned the nickname Café in honor of the coffee-colored diatoms that covered its body.

Humpbacks host a variety of internal parasites (endoparasites), including

Whales are often observed with a fish called a remora, which attaches to the host with suction cups and feed from zooplankton in the ocean as it gets a free ride.

roundworms, tapeworms, flukes, and hookworms. Young humpbacks are susceptible to a urogenital-tract ailment caused by the wormlike *Crassicauda crassicauda*. During the necropsy of a stranded two-month-old calf in Hawai'i in 1981, twelve species of internal parasites were discovered.

A variety of teleost (bony) fish and shark species including the leatherback runner (*Scombroides sancti-petri*) and

Bites from cookie cutter sharks show on this whale as white discs.

remora (*Remilegia australis*) are often observed swimming near or attached to humpbacks. They feed on bits of dead skin, algae, parasitic worms, and the small invertebrates attached to the whale's body. Many humpbacks have mysterious oval or round wounds and white scars on their heads, backs, and flanks. Since leatherback runners could not have caused such symmetrical scars it has been suggested that these markings are caused by remoras, squid, octopus, or sharks. It is likely that many of the scars result from a small nocturnal shark, *Isistius brasiliensis*, which is eighteen inches in length and has round, fleshy, suction-cup lips that allow it to attach to virtually any animal. Known as the cookie-cutter shark, it feeds by attaching to the humpback and sinking its teeth into the whale's flesh. As the whale swims, the water current and the whale's movements turn the shark slowly around, enabling it to slice out a two-inch-deep circle of flesh, leaving behind a clean, round scar.

Chapter 13

HOW LONG CAN A HUMPBACK WHALE LIVE?

One method of age determination discovered by Norwegian and Russian biologists in the 1940s is based upon annual changes in the growth rate of baleen plates. It has been determined that as the baleen plates grow through periods of feeding and fasting during each year, slight but detectable variations in their thickness occur. By counting the series of grooves and ridges across the plates, estimates were made of the age of the whales brought aboard whaling ships. Unfortunately, this method is valid only up to about six years of age, because wear at the tip of the continually growing plates makes determination unreliable beyond this stage.

A second method for determining age is to examine the reproductive organs. The ovaries of females bear a scar (corpus albicans) on the surface following the release of each egg. Biologists have shown that the rate of accumulation of these scars can be correlated with increases in body size and presumably increased age. But there is considerable variation in the age

This whale, observed multiple times over a twenty-year period off the east coast of Australia, has revealed important insights on the reproductive patterns of humpback whales. To kill her under the guise of "scientific whaling" would never have revealed the intricate patterns of her long life as a mother of many calves.

at which females first ovulate, and these scars become more difficult to differentiate in older females.

Biologists are not even certain how many ovulations occur each year. For all these reasons, counting scars allows only the determination of whether one whale is older than another but does little to tell us about the specific age of either. The age of male humpbacks has been estimated by weighing the testes in conjunction with measuring the degree of ossification of the vertebral column (as mammals age, certain vertebrae begin to fuse). This method tends to be inaccurate because a male's testes can vary widely within a year depending upon reproductive state once sexual maturity has been attained.

A third way to determine the age of a humpback is to examine its ear canals. Most mammals excrete a waxy substance from the inner car which is eventually displaced through the external ear opening. The humpback's tiny external ear opening, which prevents water from pouring in, also stops the waxy excretion from moving out. As a result, the earwax builds upon itself, forming a solid plug

that fills the auditory canal. This ear plug can attain a length of nearly three feet in adults. If the ear plug is sliced in half lengthwise, each year's layer of wax can be differentiated from the next. In fact, one is able to see alternating light and dark layers, which accrue during periods of rapid growth associated with summer feeding, and periods of slower growth caused by winter fasting. By counting the layers, or laminations, an estimate of the whale's age may be derived. Unfortunately, not all layers are clearly distinguished—especially those laid down early in life. The laminations produced in years of high food consumption are much more noticeable than those produced in leaner years. Even periods of pregnancy and lactation can influence the laminations in such a way as to make them difficult to distinguish. Consequently this is a very inexact method for determining age.

Japanese researchers have argued that by combining the various inexact methods described above, a more accurate determination of age may be made. But the central problem remains: you must kill the whale to age it. Like many,

Photographs of one whale observed repeatedly in Alaska and Hawai'i since 1976 establish that it is at least forty years of age.

we believe this to be not only unnecessary but unacceptable as well. A more recent method holds promise in determining age that does not require killing or even harming the whale. Australian scientists are developing a method of aging that has been successful in humans and may also be successful in whales. The method is based on examining telomeres, which are structures that are found on the ends of chromosomes. In many species, including humans, the telomeres become shorter as the animal ages. If the rate of change can be determined by examining whales whose ages are known, then any living whale can be aged at any time by simply examining the genetic components of sloughed skin or biopsy samples. While there is still considerable work to be done to calibrate and confirm the process, it holds great promise.

In spite of the vagaries in estimating age using the techniques available to date, the following general parameters describe life cycle development in humpbacks. Puberty is reached at about six to eight years of age, with sexual or reproductive maturity following within the next two to five years. Depending on reproductive fitness, males may take even longer to reach sexual maturity and may not ever mate. For Hawaiian humpbacks it has been estimated that females first give birth at an average of twelve years of age. Both sexes continue to grow through the early stages of adulthood, reaching physical maturity between sixteen and twenty years of age. It must be emphasized that such estimates are derived from a number of different studies based on small datasets.

Humpbacks probably to live to be fifty to sixty years of age, although the maximum age may be eighty years or longer. One female in the South Pacific was estimated to be at least fifty years of age at the time she was killed. This brings us back to the original point that methods of age determination used in the past seem of little value today because they are dependent upon killing the whale. The current use of photographic identification and genetic techniques will allow more refined conclusions about the development of life histories of known individuals. This will lead to more precise answers to questions about age while leaving the population unharmed. The oldest humpback whale in the North Pacific documented by photographic identification was first photographed in 1972 and then photographed both in Alaska and in Hawai'i on several occasions, with the last known photograph taken in 2006. Since it appeared to be an adult at time of first sighting, we know this animal is at least forty years of age.

Chapter 14

NO TWO HUMPBACKS LOOK ALIKE

In the early 1950s biologists studying large whales off the East Coast of the United States claimed they could resight individuals based on scars and markings on their bodies. In the early 1970s Chuck Jurasz, working in southeast Alaska, began identifying individual humpback whales based on photographs of the distinct patterns of black-and-white markings on the underside of the tail flukes. In 1979 Steve Katona and his colleagues, working off the New England coast, established that these conspicuous coloration patterns are unique to each animal and are of special importance in long-term tracking studies of free-living whales. They noted that, as with the human fingerprint, no two whales possess the same fluke print. Ventral fluke coloration varies from all white to all black, with an infinite variety of mottled black-and-white patterns in between (see page

The coloration and marking pattern of the ventral surface of each whale's tail is unique to that animal.

109). Many animals also have permanent scars on their flukes caused by shark and orca attacks, from scraping against rocks, or from cuts from barnacles attached to other whales. Whales are also seen with wounds, cuts, holes, and even large portions of the tail missing as a result of collisions with vessels and entanglements with fishing gear and marine debris.

When a humpback dives after a series of respirations at the surface, it frequently lifts its tail out of the water in a "fluke-up dive" (see page 132), revealing the pattern on the ventral surface of the tail. Photographs of the ventral portion of the tail can be compiled into a catalog of fluke identifications complete with information about the sighting (date, time, pod composition, travel direction, presence or absence of a calf, and so on). These fluke photographs are instrumental in yielding new insights into migratory routes, population estimates, social structure and behavior, longevity, sexual maturity, and reproductive rate, and, most important, remove the need to kill whales in order to study and understand them. The tail patterns of newborn calves are less distinct and are not established until

Deformities such as missing portions of the fluke (top) or holes in the fluke, and marks from barnacles (bottom) provide unique patterns that help identify individual animals.

they reach the feeding ground. In addition, newborn calves show their flukes less when submerging. This has made it difficult to identify individual calves on the breeding grounds.

Calves seldom show the ventral portion of the fluke when diving, but when they do, the milky coloration and dark markings show the early hints of unique markings that will allow individual identification.

Prior to the 1970s research scientists tracked humpback whales using numbered stainless-steel darts known as Discovery Tags. These darts were fired into the dorsal musculature to be recovered during processing after the whale was killed. Whaling biologists operating in the Southern Hemisphere during the first half of the century shot nearly five thousand Discovery Tags into humpbacks. Fewer than 3 percent were ever recovered. Even those provided no information about movements of animals during the period between marking by scientists and capture by the whaling ships. Most often the animals were killed not far from the original marking spot, often within days or weeks of being tagged. Determination of specific migratory routes was next to impossible as there was no way to establish whether the animal had ever left the area even after months or years passed between marking and capture.

Many attempts have been made to develop long-term, visible tags for large whales. These include branding (impractical for large species which cannot be handled easily), streamer tags (often dislodged by water turbulence), and dye (it usually washes away). Since the 1980s radio-tagging has been employed with success on a number of large and small cetaceans and is still being used to track animals near shore throughout nighttime and daylight hours. Radio-tagging is limited in the duration of time and distance over which individuals can be tracked. By attaching electronic data recorders to the tags, additional information on dive profiles, respiration rates, vocalizations, ambient sounds, and foraging patterns can be obtained with considerable accuracy.

These tags are either mounted on the dorsal fin, anchored subcutaneously, or attached by a suction cup. There are a

Fluke patterns may range from nearly all white to virtually all dark.

number of intrinsic drawbacks associated with each type of tag used. To be useful, a tag must meet a number of criteria:

1. The tag should not cause significant physical damage or hinder the animal's natural movement.
2. The tag should not cause the animal to become isolated from or avoided by conspecifics or make it more attractive to predators.
3. The tag should remain in place for a predetermined period of time and then detach cleanly and easily.
4. The tag should be easy to recover.

Technical problems such as short battery life, equipment failure, and difficulty receiving and transmitting broadcast signals have sometimes limited the use of radio tags to date. Technological advances in the reduction of size and weight of the transmitters, however, combined with increased access to satellites, have improved tracking techniques and the quality of data gathered.

In recent years, through the efforts like those of the National Geographic Society, a number of marine animal species have been outfitted with small, high-quality underwater video cameras. This innovative technology has provided some new insights on prolonged interactions within pods of whales. Researchers are also trying to obtain more sustained observations of animals through the use of above-surface mechanized platforms such as airships, remotely controlled drones, and high-altitude aircraft. The digital age allows remote, noninvasive viewing techniques that are highly efficient and of high resolution. Coupled with sophisticated computer programming, huge datasets can be searched, analyzed, and interpreted with far greater speed and accuracy than has ever been possible. New technologies are constantly being derived from military operations such as forward-looking radar, infrared and heat detectors, and acoustic monitoring devices. These techniques allow for remotely controlled, twenty-four-hour monitoring of whales over all the oceans of the world, whether the animals are at the surface or below it.

We have been observers of, and participants in, an amazing series of changes in the way information about humpback whales is collected. When we began studying humpback whales, there were still biologists working on whaling ships, trying to understand live whales by studying dead ones. Today there are researchers who can use sophisticated technology controlled from laboratories and computer rooms, who never even have to see a whale in order to figure out where it is and what it may be doing. While these advances are truly beneficial, we believe that ultimately, in order to know what a whale is and how it makes its living, you need to spend time on the ocean, face-to-fluke with these magnificent animals,

Tail fluke identification research allows a great deal of information to be collected over extended periods of time with virtually no disturbance to the whale.

Humpback whales may also be identified by unique dorsal fin shape and body coloration and marking patterns. We have identified four lateral body coloration patterns ranging from Type I (top) to Type IV (bottom).

to properly gauge not just their biology but also their greater significance in our increasingly threatened planet.

Humpbacks may also be identified on the basis of dorsal fin shape and body scarring. Dorsal fins of humpback whales come in an endless variety of shapes, ranging from high, curved fins to inconspicuous bumps. Photographs of the right and left views of the dorsal fin can help to identify whales when no fluke photograph is available. Such identification is made difficult by the changing appearance of the dorsal fin as the whale rounds out and dives. Quite often the job is easier when the dorsal fin is heavily scarred on one or both sides, or in rare cases where part of the fin has been notched or removed. Body scars obtained from contact with rocks, anchor lines, ships' bows, sharks, orcas, fellow humpbacks, and other cetaceans are like tattoos that can be used to identify individual whales.

Humpback whales also display variations in black-and-white patterns on the ventral and lateral surfaces of their body. We have defined four lateral body pigmentation types for humpbacks ranging from nearly all white to all black. While we have observed all four body types in our research in the Southern Hemisphere, whales in Hawai'i have little or no white markings on their sides. The coloration pattern of the pectoral fins is generally not used in the identification process, although they are subject to a great deal of scarring. In general, the pectoral fins are not as easy to observe as the dorsal fin and tail. Nonetheless, special notations are made in the fluke catalog when a whale has distinct pectoral fins, such as a unique scar, white coloration, or conspicuous damage.

Although patterns in pigmentation, scars, and dorsal-fin shape are useful in discovering the life history of individual animals, they do not indicate the whale's sex. By taking skins samples from animals and using the genetic techniques described earlier, information about the whale's sex, relatedness patterns, and possibly age can be obtained. Material for analysis is collected by firing a hollow, six-inch biopsy dart into a surfacing whale's side. The dart is constructed so that immediately after penetrating the whale it bounces out into the water where it can be retrieved. A small core sample of tissue is embedded in the tip. This tissue is frozen and stored so that it can later be stained and cytologically tested.

There are few easily noticed differences in male and female external appearance. The most notable differences are found on the ventral surface. The distance between the genital opening and the anus is almost two and a half times greater in males than in females. The genital opening of males is more anterior than that of females. On the posterior end of the female's genital slit is a grapefruit-size swelling called the hemispherical lobe. Underwater photographs of the lateral or ventral views of a humpback clearly show the hemispherical lobe in the female and its absence in males (see photos, pages 51-52). This technique is an important discovery, but it is far from an easy procedure. Taking a picture of the genital opening of a humpback whale is like lying on a highway trying to get a photograph of the oil pan of a semitrailer truck as it passes overhead.

Diagram of the genital area of a male and female humpback whale (after Glockner).

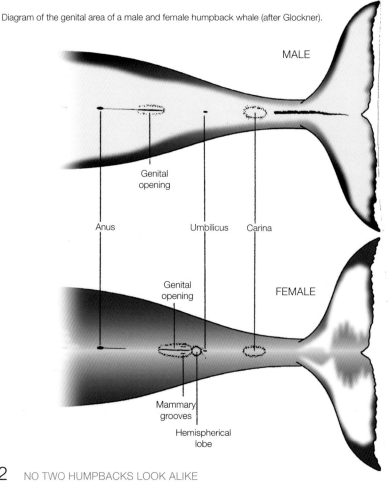

MALE

Genital
opening

Anus   Umbilicus   Carina

Genital
opening   FEMALE

Mammary
grooves

Hemispherical
lobe

Chapter 15

HOW WHALES COMMUNICATE

Humpback whales have had to develop a method of communication suited to their environment. At depths vision becomes limited, and calling over the tops of waves while at the surface can be extremely energy consuming. Sound travels five to six times faster underwater than in air, with low frequencies traveling the farthest. The precise speed at which sound travels in water is a function of temperature, salinity, turbidity, and depth. The increased speed of sound in water makes it an ideal form of communication for cetaceans. While all cetaceans are able to emit sounds under a variety of conditions, the humpback whale seems unique among baleen species in the complex diversity of its underwater vocalizations. No one has yet accurately measured the distance across which humpback whales can communicate effectively. Theoretical modeling has established that, under ideal conditions, some humpback whale sounds can travel hundreds, if not thousands, of kilometers.

Body posture and coloration can provide visual signals for communication at close range.

SONG SESSION
A humpback whale's song is made of multiple themes

THEME			
PHRASE		**PHRASE**	
SUBPHRASE	SUBPHRASE	SUBPHRASE	SUBPHRASE
UNITS UNITS	UNITS UNITS	UNITS UNITS	UNITS UNITS

The humpback whale's song is comprised of a highly structured sequence of vocalizations.

Humpbacks produce a wide array of sounds, including the highest and the lowest frequencies humans can hear, with an extraordinary range of tonal qualities. Researchers in Australia have recently identified more than thirty distinct sound types. Sound types are differentiated on the basis of a variety of elements such as frequency range, duration, where the peak energy falls in the vocalization, and amplitude pattern. It appears that both males and females can produce the full range of sound types. This has important implications for considering whether or not humpback communication patterns have languagelike features. An important characteristic of a "true language" is that all members of the species are able to produce relevant, meaningful units of sound and are able not only to produce them but also to comprehend them. While we are a long way from fully understanding the communication capabilities of humpback whales, there is growing evidence that whether their sounds form a true language or not, the production and structure of these sounds suggests at least some simple languagelike functions.

How humpbacks create these sounds is unknown, since they do not have functional vocal cords. The sounds are most likely produced by various

How humpback whales produce sound is unknown, since they do not have functional vocal cords.

Although both males and females are capable of making a wide variety of vocalizations, only the males produce the complex sequences of sounds called songs.

valves, muscles, and a series of blind sacs found branching off the respiratory tract. O. W. Schreiber was the first to report humpback whale sounds, in 1952, based on recordings collected at the U.S. Navy Sound Fixing and Ranging Station (SOFAR) in Kāneʻohe Bay, Hawaiʻi. In 1958 Alex Kibblewhite, working for the New Zealand Navy, described similar sounds as the "barnyard chorus," and noted their coincidence with the annual migration of humpback whales through New Zealand waters. In 1967 Frank Watlington, a U.S. Naval acoustic engineer, made recordings of humpback whale sounds he had collected in Bermuda available to biologist Roger Payne, who later reported with Scott McVay that the sounds of humpback

whales were organized into repeating patterns, which they described as songs. Soon after, Katy Payne found that the humpback song displayed a characteristic without precedent among nonhumans. It showed a constant and progressive change from year to year, unlike the songs of birds.

A humpback song is composed of a series of discrete notes or units. A unit is the shortest discrete sound noticeable to the human ear. A series of units constitutes a phrase. Phrases are usually uniform in duration, and may contain repeated sounds. A consecutive group of phrases make up a theme. Although a given theme may vary in the number of phrases it contains, the sequence of its phrases is always the same. Similarly the sequence in which themes occur never varies, although some themes may be left out. A predictable series of themes forms a song. A song generally lasts between six and eighteen minutes, depending on the number of phrases it includes. A sequence of songs separated by brief pauses constitutes a song session. The length and number of singing bouts increase as the season progresses, with the maximum number of singers being heard during the latter half of the breeding season. Song sessions can be highly variable in duration. Some animals stop singing after a few minutes. On the other hand, whales may engage in protracted song sessions. We once listened to a whale in Hawai'i sing near-continuously for fourteen hours before we had to head into shore under darkness. The whale was still singing when we left it.

The whale's song is in a constant state of evolution. As the season progresses, new themes may be introduced or old ones may be changed. Each singer changes its song to keep in tune with other singers. As a result the song heard at the end of the season is quite different from the song heard at the beginning. Little or no singing takes place during the summer, and further change to the song does not

appear to occur. When the whales return to Hawai'i the following winter, they resume singing the version in vogue at the end of the previous breeding season. The song continues to change as years go by. After five years the song is hardly recognizable compared to its earlier form. To date, song components that have been dropped have never reappeared.

We now know that all the whales in a given breeding area sing the same song. Although similar units may occur in songs from different parts of the world, the song performed within a breeding area has its own unique set of themes and phrases. In the North Pacific we have seen that whales in the breeding areas of Hawai'i, Japan, and Mexico have shared theme components, but the song is unique to each area. Photographic identification of flukes has established that a small number of whales switch breeding grounds in different years. Whales seen in Japan or the Philippines in one winter may show up in Hawai'i or Mexico in another winter. This may help explain how songs across these widely separate areas may share some components. What is not clear is how this sharing of components may occur within a season. One possibility is that whales may also move across widely distant breeding

This tail fluke identifies a male that travelled between Mexico and Hawaii in the same winter, covering nearly three thousand miles in 51 days.

areas within the same winter. Working with colleagues from Mexico, we found one incident of a male humpback that traveled from Mexico to Hawai'i within in the same winter breeding season. It traveled some twenty-eight hundred miles in fifty-one days. Another possibility is that the song is learned on the feeding grounds or during migration where animals from different breeding areas may mix and the occasional song is heard.

Scientists working in Australia have shown that humpback whales off the east coast incorporated elements of the western Australia song over a two-year period. The two populations are quite distinct and to date only a handful of incidents suggest interchange. A colleague in western Australia has matched one of his photos obtained offshore of Perth, on the west coast, with an animal we identified in Hervey Bay, on the east coast of Australia. Even isolated occurrences of interchange may have significant impact on the development of song.

Kenneth Norris proposed in 1966 that because singing occurs primarily during the breeding season, the song serves a reproductive function. The exact way in which it is used to accomplish this is unknown. Females have been heard emitting what have been described as song fragments but it is overwhelmingly the case that song is a male behavior. A number of hypotheses have been proposed with regard to song's function. It may attract females, scare away other males, or maintain the distance between singers. Some have suggested that, much like chorusing in frogs, the combined effect of singing males may synchronize ovulation in females. Others believe the song display allows animals to either find each other or assess the location and distance at which potential rivals may be located. An interesting and more recent claim is that the song may be a mechanism for coordinating the behaviors of male cohorts in out-competing rivals in the effort to stay close to, and mate with, ovulating females.

We believe that a behavior as energetically demanding as the song display may not only serve a number of functions, but also that its occurrence in the life of a particular individual may be developmentally differentiated. Not all singers are of the same age, the same fitness, nor do they experience the same level of success. Even with regard to mature animals that may be successful, the number of available females can differ greatly across the breeding season. In some cases a singer may simply be a young, inexperienced animal practicing to hold his breath longer, sing more loudly, or incorporate new elements of the song to increase chances of mating success. At other times, when relatively few males may be around, there may be less need to use the song as a competitive device. As more males show up there may well be increased pressure to either challenge,

While we do not know the exact function of the song, it is a complex display that serves an important role in male mating behaviors.

warn, or threaten other males. At some point, presumably near the peak of the breeding season, a maximum number of males and a relatively fewer number of receptive females creates a situation in which cooperation of alliances of males may be advantageous. There may also be males of reproductive age who have failed to mate but persist in singing in the off chance that they may get the opportunity. The alternative hypotheses may not be mutually exclusive. There is yet insufficient evidence to allow a forceful and full portrayal of the role song plays in the life of male humpback whales. Our point is that singing may occur for a variety of reasons at various times: practice, competition, cooperation, and simple persistence may characterize the behavior of any particular male throughout the breeding season.

Although singing is a distinctly male behavior, when the opportunity to mate arises, "it takes two to tango." Humpback females can mate with a number of males within a breeding season. The female cost of bearing and raising offspring is tremendous. It is to the female's advantage to mate only with the most fit males. A great deal of effort to date has gone into understanding the function of the song and the behaviors of the male in breeding activities. We know virtually nothing about the mechanisms available to females to

ensure they mate with the best possible male. It is the females, however, that are the limiting resource. Ultimately a much better understanding of female behavior during the breeding season is required to properly understand the function of the song in the context of both female and male mating strategies.

Most frequently the male is alone and remains in the same general location during the song session. Singing whales have been observed, however, in pods of two or three males, in large active pods containing a female, and with mothers and calves. We have observed whales singing in Hawai'i, Fiji, Ecuador, Japan, American Samoa, Tonga, and Australia. A lone singing whale rests head-down some fifty to seventy-five feet below the surface. With its eyes closed and its tail pointed skyward, it remains motionless save for the slow movement of the pectoral fins forward and back, looking much like an opera singer swinging his arms to help hit those high and low notes. A singer typically stays down for fifteen minutes or so, although durations as long as an hour sometimes occur. It will then surface within two hundred yards of its last surface location. As it rises to the surface, a noticeable attenuation in the song occurs, making it possible to determine when the whale is about to surface and blow.

Observing a singing whale underwater is an impressive experience. In the deep clear waters of Hawai'i, the sunlight creates shafts of light that make the whale appear to be on the stage of some huge blue theater in which you are the only audience. The rich tonal qualities of the song seem to completely envelop you. The song is produced with such strength and power that it literally resonates through your body. Recent estimates of the source level of the humpback whale song have measured at approximately 180 decibels. Although on land this equates to the sound of a jet

engine, underwater the mass of the ocean creates sufficient insulation to prevent permanent damage to the human ear. The experience of being next to a singing whale is like standing beside the pipes of an organ in a massive cathedral.

We have also observed singing male humpbacks escorting mothers with calves. On one of these occasions the escort continued to sing as the trio moved along the shoreline. The song was so loud we could hear it above the outboard engine as we traveled slowly along behind them. On another occasion, one of us was in the water with a mother and calf when a male escort whale suddenly swam beneath and began to sing! It seems paradoxical that a reproductively active male would approach a mother and calf. Lactating females normally do not ovulate and are therefore probably not receptive to mating. Perhaps those males that approach mothers and calves are young animals still learning about the context in which it is appropriate to sing and which females may be receptive. Alternatively they could be older animals that have not been successful in mating and are approaching mothers with calves in what may be thought of as a last, desperate act. Such approaches may not be totally unwarranted. It has been estimated that the mortality rate of neonate humpback whales may be as high as 30 percent. Females known to have given birth in successive years are thought to have ovulated after losing a newborn calf. Approaching a mother with a newborn calf may not after all be a completely lost cause if the calf, for one reason or another, has stopped nursing.

There are also situations in which singers are approached by what appear to be males, who at times may be singers themselves. Sometimes these pods then approach larger groups of animals competing for access to a female. These incidents seem most frequent at the peak of the season when competition by males for access to females is most intense. It remains to be seen whether these interactions may be characterized as either competitive or cooperative.

It is important to realize that humpback whale song is not as stereotypical or genetically controlled as the song of many bird or reptile species. There is increasing evidence that individual males may alter the duration of the song depending on the distance to the intended recipient. At close range it is advantageous to cycle through as many song displays as possible. When the recipient is at some distance, however, much of the signal in the song will be lost. The strategy then becomes increasing the broadcast effectiveness of the song by repeating its low-frequency elements, because low-frequency sounds travel farther underwater. Researchers have found that it is possible to tell how far away a sound source is underwater based on predictable changes in the sound with increasing distance. It is not yet certain whether whales use such information, but the possibility is intriguing.

There is little doubt that the song is an important form of communication. Exactly what is communicated remains in question. These days singing whales can be tracked and observed twenty-four hours a day and from considerable distances through the use of remotely monitored hydrophones. This has resulted in the determination that singing may actually be more frequent at night that during the daytime. The present status of acoustic analysis is such that it is possible to identify individual singers based on acoustic characteristics. The location and rate of movement of individual animals may be pinpointed by triangulation of the sound source. Further elaboration of these techniques may allow us to not only know where the sounds are being made and who is making them, but also what they mean.

Newborn calves engage in a variety of relatively simple, brief social sounds n the vicinity of their mothers.

Humpbacks make other vocalizations and sounds that are associated with a wide range of social contexts such as feeding, parental care, and courtship activity. Such social sounds are made by males and females alike and do not appear to be characterized by the elaborate patterns and complex organization found in the song. The sound units found in the song include those used as social sounds. What is unique about the song is not the sound units themselves but the patterns in which they occur. Social sounds seem to function in much the same way as the vocalizations of other mammals, serving to communicate messages of biological urgency. We have observed vocalizations between mothers and calves during underwater observations in both Hawai'i and Australia. Researchers working in Hawai'i recently recorded these sounds. They report that the sounds made by calves are fairly limited in number and include "grunts, bubbles, and squeaks." The sounds are of limited duration and relatively simple in acoustic structure. Calves are more likely to make sounds when accompanied only by their mothers than when in larger groups. We believe that mothers may communicate with their calves using infrasonic sounds below the threshold of human hearing. Our observations of calves suddenly moving back towards their mothers, and mother-calf pods actively avoiding each other at a distance of a quarter mile or so, have occurred in the absence of detectable sounds. The use of low-frequency hydrophones and recording equipment will confirm our suspicion. Continued observations of mothers and calves could tell us much about the importance of learning and imitation in the development of vocalization capabilities.

Chapter 16

USING SONAR TO SEE

Toothed whales and dolphins communicate with sound and also use these abilities to echolocate or scan the underwater environment. Echolocation involves producing very-high-frequency sounds that can be transmitted over relatively long distances. The sounds strike objects in the water (for example, fish, land formations, flotsam and jetsam, or ocean flora). The echo from the sound returns to the transmitting animal and provides information about the nature of the object. Dolphins also whistle to communicate with each other. There is some evidence that individuals in certain species have signature whistles by which they are able to identify each other. Communicative social sounds may be used for group contact, cohesion, and socializing, but all are still poorly understood by humans.

In odontocetes echolocation sounds are produced in air sacs attached to the respiratory tract, and are directed through fatty deposits in the forehead (the "melon"). The sounds are produced in pulses, so that as the echo from each pulse returns, the animal is able to compare it with the outgoing pulses. The time lag between the two provides the animal with information about the distance to the object, the size of the object, its shape, and even the material from which it is made. Most of these echolocation sounds are beyond the frequencies of human hearing. Some people can hear clicking sounds when whales or dolphins echolocate. These clicking sounds are the only frequencies of the pulsed sounds audible to humans. Only odontocetes have been confirmed to possess the ability to echolocate. Phocid seals have been recorded producing

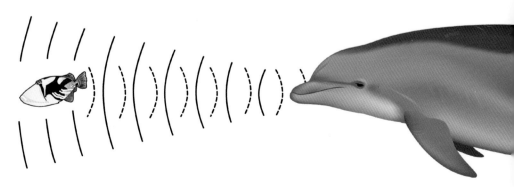

Humpback whales do not make the ultra-high frequency sounds that odontocetes do, and are therefore not thought capable of echolocation.

underwater clicks that are probably used for echolocation; this has not been proven, however, and is currently being debated in the research community.

Baleen whales, including humpbacks, do not make the ultra-high-frequency sounds necessary for active biosonar, or echolocation. It is possible that they may use echoes returning from low-frequency sounds in a less sophisticated way (termed "passive listening") to detect the presence of objects close by. Acoustic specialists working off the East Coast of the United States have recorded the occurrences of unique sounds made by humpback whales they termed "megaclicks." They report clicks occur only at night and near the seafloor and are associated with feeding. Although much lower in frequency, the sounds are similar in structure to the echolocation sounds of toothed-whales. So little is known about the hearing system of humpbacks that it is difficult to conclude they are in fact echolocation sounds.

Chapter 17
A GUIDE TO BEHAVIORS

In the following guide to behaviors, we first list general activities displayed by groups, and then specific behaviors displayed by individual animals. Individual behaviors are further categorized according to the body part involved. Several of the terms are self-explanatory; others are more obscure. While some were coined by whalers of days gone by, scientists have developed other terms more recently in order to specify more exactly the wide range of behaviors of interest.

We first published this list of behaviors in 1986. In 1989 we were invited to the Ogasawara islands in Japan to consult with the local community as they transitioned from whale hunting to whalewatching. While standing atop a headland with a group of local guides watching whales just offshore, we initially felt somewhat lost without translation. Suddenly however we began to recognize occasional phrases in English and realized they had all memorized the terms from our list of behaviors. Since then we have worked with government agencies, educational organizations, the whalewatching industry, and other researchers to make these terms a universal language among watchers of humpback whales. In some areas we have seen terms adapted to the local dialect. In Australia what we call "spy hopping" has become "peepholing." We also recognize that as the terms have promoted more and more observation, they have sometimes been refined or redefined to more subtly and accurately capture the incredible range of humpback whale behaviors. We have tried to incorporate some of these changes in the list presented here.

Development of a well-defined list of identifiable displays and behaviors (such as this peduncle slap) helps scientists understand the complex social patterns of the animals being studied.

©M&M Sweet

GROUP ACTIVITY

POD FORMATION: "Pod" is a term used to describe whales that appear to be in close proximity to one another (within two or three body-lengths) and apparently engaged in related behaviors. A pod may include only a single whale. Use of the term is, of course, from the human observer's perspective. We do not know for certain what constitutes a coherent group from the humpback whale's point of view.

SLOW-MEDIUM-FAST SWIM: A slow swim for a humpback is anything slower than two to three miles per hour, a medium swim from three to eight miles per hour, and a fast swim anything faster than eight miles per hour. Speeds of more than eight miles per hour occur for relatively short periods of time. During migration, humpbacks usually swim at a medium pace, or between three and eight miles per hour. While a single animal or a small group of two to three whales may engage in dedicated swimming for a prolonged period of time, large groups of whales generally intersperse bouts of swimming with periods of high-energy activity.

SURFACE ACTIVITY: Pods of two or more whales may often engage in a number of high-energy behaviors while visible above the surface. Surface-active pods may display a variety of individual behaviors while remaining under way. Normally, surfacing intervals and locations are highly predictable. Swimming speed and direction can be effected by the presence of boats, aircraft, and other whales. Surfacing bouts appear to involve all the whales in a group, although not all whales will necessarily surface at exactly the same time;

part of the group may surface and blow, with the remainder surfacing immediately after the first animals submerge. This can often make it difficult to determine the exact number of whales in a group if there are more than four or five and observations are being made from a boat.

MILLING: A group of whales remains at the surface for an extended period of time, with no apparent progress in a specific direction. Whales may engage in a wide range of activities, from the rather sedate to highly charged, while milling.

RESTING: "Resting" is a term usually applied to a mother and calf, although we have observed as many as eight whales quietly "logging" at the surface. Often the whale's back can be seen throughout the resting episode, although on many occasions the whale may slowly submerge after rising to the surface to breathe and remain hidden below the water before surfacing again in the same location some time later.

AFFILIATION/DISAFFILIATION: Humpbacks in Hawai'i, with the exception of mother-calf pairs, generally form very transient, apparently short-lived groups. Whales are said to affiliate when they come together to interact, however briefly, and to disaffiliate when the interaction is terminated and one or more whales leave the pod for at least fifteen minutes. Escort whales will affiliate with and disaffiliate from a series of mother-calf pods rather than remain with the same one for longer than a few hours.

INDIVIDUAL BEHAVIORS

RESPIRATION

BLOW: Breathing occurs through the paired blowhole openings on the top of the head. The term refers to both the act of normal exhalation and inhalation at the surface and the cloud of water droplets produced above the animal's head during the process of exhalation.

NO-BLOW RISE: Often the humpback will surface without making an audible blow, or producing the characteristic plumelike cloud. Such a silent surfacing is referred to as a "no-blow rise."

UNDERWATER BLOW: Humpbacks do not always wait until their blowholes clear the surface before they exhale. Whales that are moving at relatively fast speeds or surfacing and diving quickly will frequently begin to exhale just before their head breaks the surface, creating a small explosion of frothing water.

BUBBLING: Humpbacks often release controlled amounts of air from the blowholes or even the mouth while underwater. (It is generally assumed that air released from the mouth has been "gulped" at the surface, since humpbacks do not breathe through their mouths.) Such "bubbling" takes a variety of forms:

BUBBLE BLAST: A "bubble blast" is a sudden explosive release of air through the blowholes while the whale is completely underwater, often in proximity to another whale.

BUBBLE TRAIL: A "bubble trail" is created by the release of air from the blowholes or mouth while the whale is still underwater. The trail begins at the blowhole openings or corners of the mouth as two distinct lines, which quickly fuse into a chain of small bubbles stretching out fifty yards or more behind the whale.

BUBBLE SCREEN: A "bubble screen" is a controlled, intermittent release of air from the blowholes while the whale is underwater, which results in a thick cloud of small bubbles less than a quarter inch in diameter. This differs from a bubble trail in that the bubbles are localized in a contained, relatively small area.

BUBBLE NET: A "bubble net" is the controlled, underwater release of air from the blowholes carried out while the whale swims or turns in a circle of approximately thirty to forty feet in diameter. The bubbles of air rise to the surface and burst, forming a spiraling trail. This is a behavior associated with feeding activity and is observed in its most distinct form only on the Alaskan feeding grounds (see Chapter 10, Finding Food).

POSTURES

ROUND OUT/PEDUNCLE ARCH/SLIP UNDER: Whales often breathe more than once after surfacing, often as many as three to five times within a brief, two- or three-minute period. Following the last inhalation, the whale begins a diving descent by arching its body slightly while rolling ahead at the surface. This is referred to as the "round out." As the caudal peduncle appears at the surface, the whale may arch it high above the water, perhaps in an attempt to dive more deeply. This is called the "peduncle arch". If the whale submerges without rounding out or arching the peduncle or both, it is called a "slip under".

FLUKE-UP DIVE/FLUKE-DOWN DIVE: Following a peduncle arch, the humpback will usually bring its tail flukes above the surface of the water as it dives almost straight down. In a "fluke-up dive" (below left) the entire ventral surface of the flukes will be exposed, showing the unique pattern of markings found on each whale. In a "fluke-down dive" (below right) the flukes are brought clear of the water, but remain turned down, so the ventral surface is not exposed. In Hawai'i adults frequently do fluke-up dives; calves generally do not.

SNAKING: Whales in surface-active groups sometimes engage in an S-shaped postural display we have termed "snaking." In this posture, the anterior portion of the head is angled up out of the water, the dorsal fin is just above the surface, the peduncle is arched just below the water, and the flukes may be kept underwater or exposed. It seems a very peculiar, almost impossible, posture for a large whale to assume. This unusual behavior is done while the whale is swimming at the surface, and is held only briefly. Both dolphins and sharks have been observed in similar behavior while fully underwater and it is thought to be an aggressive display.

MOTORBOATING: The whale swims rapidly at the surface with its head angled above the water with the rest of the body parallel to the surface. As the whale moves along in this position, the head creates a visible wake much like that created by the hull of a boat moving through the water. This is sometimes accompanied by a bubble trail.

DORSAL WOBBLE: While a whale is at the surface with its back exposed, a noticeable tremor in the dorsal fin may occur. Whales that display this "dorsal wobble" do not do so at every surfacing, suggesting that there may be direct or indirect voluntary control of the dorsal fin movement. The display is observed more often in surface-active groups.

HEAD DISPLAYS

SPY HOP: The whale rises relatively straight up out of the water rather slowly, maintains its head above the surface so the eye is just above or just below the surface, often turns 90° to 180° on its longitudinal axis, then slips back below the surface.

HEAD RISE: The head is brought up above the surface of the water at a 45° to 90° angle. Generally the eye is not exposed. The mouth may sometimes be partially inflated.

HEAD LUNGE/INFLATED HEAD LUNGE: The head is brought above the surface of the water at a 0° to 45° angle while the whale lunges forward with a momentary burst of speed. Often the humpback will expand or inflate its mouth by filling it with water, perhaps in an attempt to increase its apparent size. The display is often carried out broadside to another whale.

HEAD SLAP: The "head slap" is an exciting display of the humpback's power and size. Propelling half of its body out of the water nearly perpendicularly, the whale pounds its massive, sometimes partially engorged mouth back down onto the water's surface, sending out explosions of water around its head. The head will rise fifteen feet or so above the water at the peak of the display. Some have referred to the head slap as a "breach" or "incomplete breach," but we reserve the term "breach" for another behavior that we believe to be functionally distinct from the head slap.

HEAD BUTT: Male humpback whales use their ponderous, oversized heads to push each other out of the way as they jostle for position in the pod. The male humpback rises out of the water beside another whale and then forces the ventral surface of his head down on the dorsal surface of the competitor's head. It has been suggested that the jaw plate on the end of the lower jaw, which is often encrusted with barnacles, may be used to enhance the effect of the maneuver. Whales on the receiving end of such attacks end up with their head scarred and bleeding, especially on the surface of the sensory nodules.

HEAD SHAKE: Both above and below the water's surface, humpbacks display a behavior that has been seen in many species of dolphins, and is associated with threatening. The whale (as with the dolphin) shakes its head quickly from side to side while swimming toward another whale. Cetaceans, with few exceptions, have fused neck vertebrae, making the side-to-side movement look much like a quick and violent twitch or jerk.

JAW CLAP: Humpbacks signal stress, and perhaps anger, by a violent clapping of the lower jaw against the upper jaw. In competitive groups individuals may first head-lunge and then quickly "jaw-clap." Calves are also capable of jaw clapping, and we have observed them doing so as they repeatedly breached. Jaw clapping may occur above or below the surface.

EYE WIDENING: The humpback's eye is not usually fully visible. Generally, it does not clear the surface of the water long enough to be observed in air, and from a distance it is obscured by thick folds of skin which almost completely cover it. Underwater the eye appears only as a darkened opening in these folds. On occasion, however, the eye appears to bulge and widen, exposing the white around the iris. In dolphins, such

"eye widening" is a sure sign of stress induced by either fear or anger, and it is likely that the same is true of the humpback. This behavior occurs underwater, and would be seen by most people only in underwater photographs and film footage.

PECTORAL FIN DISPLAYS

PEC RUBBING: "Pec Rubbing" refers to the rubbing or stroking along the body of another whale with the pectoral fins. In courting pods observed from the air, one humpback may swim through the extended pectoral fins of a second whale lying on its side. Such encounters involve extensive contact with the pectoral fins. We have even observed a subadult humpback directing such behaviors at a singularly unimpressed northern right whale.

PEC EXTENSION/PEC WAVE: While the whale is lying at the surface, either on its back or side, it will often extend its pectoral fins high up into the air. Sometimes the whale will simply hold one pectoral fin, or flipper, straight up while lying on its side, with the end of one side of the fluke also exposed. (Whalewatchers may mistake the exposed portion of the fluke for the pectoral fin of a second animal). At other times, the whale will lie on its back and wave both pectoral fins back and forth in the air.

PEC SLAP: Humpbacks frequently roll at the surface, slapping their long pectoral fins against the water, or they may lie on their side, bringing one fin high up into the air and then swinging it forcefully down onto the surface of the water with a resounding smack. We have also observed whales lying on their back waving both fins in the air at the same time, before slapping them on top of the water. In general, it does not appear that "pec-slapping" is an aggressive activity, and may actually be an invitational display.

TAIL (FLUKE) DISPLAYS

TAIL WAVE/FLUKE EXTENSION: In this display the flukes and caudal peduncle are extended straight up into the air, with the animal's head pointed directly toward the ocean floor. The flukes may be gently waved back and forth ("tail wave") or simply held motionless in the air ("fluke extension").

TAIL COCK: While the whale is lying upright in the water (that is, with its dorsal surface exposed), the caudal peduncle is bent and slightly arched so that it is exposed above the surface at its posterior extremity while the flukes are bent downward, giving the impression of a slingshot about to be released. This behavior occurs while the whale is stationary at the surface.

TAIL SLASH: While the whale is lying upright or on its side at the surface it moves its flukes forcefully side to side. A lateral bending of the caudal peduncle controls the movement of the flukes.

TAIL SLAP: While the whale is lying either dorsal-up or ventral-up in the water, it forcefully slaps its flukes against the surface of the water in a "tail slap." In order to maintain stability, the whale extends its pectoral fins to either side, just below the surface. With its head completely underwater, it raises its peduncle and flukes as high up out of the water as it can, and then smashes them forcefully down, creating an explosion of water and sound.

PEDUNCLE SLAP OR THROW: In this highly aggressive behavior, the rear portion of the body, including the caudal peduncle and the flukes, is thrown up out of the water and then brought down sideways, either on the surface of the water or on top of another whale. This constitutes one of the most intensive forms of aggression in humpback whales.

FULL BODY DISPLAYS

BREACH: A "breach" is a spectacular display in which the whale propels itself out of the water, generally clearing the surface with two-thirds of its body or more. As the whale rises above the water, it throws one pectoral fin out to the side and turns in the air about its longitudinal axis. The reentry splash from a breach is comprised of two distinct parts. A relatively widespread explosion of water is created as the whale hits the surface. As the force of landing carries the whale beneath the water, a second, geyserlike plume of water rises up within the middle of the primary explosion.

LAZY BREACH: In the less spectacular "lazy breach," less than half the whale clears the surface at less than a 45° angle. The pectoral fin may often be extended, and the reentry splash is far less forceful than in a breach. This display may also be called a "half breach" or "incomplete breach."

Chapter 18
WHY WHALES DO THAT

The information we present has grown out of our conviction that people going out to see and learn about whales deserve more than to either have their questions ignored or briefly responded to with textbook answers. We think it is important to explain whale behavior not just as a list of facts but also as a web of observations that reveal a complex and exciting life lived in an environment that is so foreign to humans. We witnessed firsthand the inexperience of so-called naturalists in the early days of whalewatching in Hawai'i. We recognize that a good naturalist, guide, or interpreter knows how to plan and structure his or her presentation in a way that is based on an accurate understanding of the subject matter and responds to the needs and interest level of the participants. The challenge is to tell a good story, make sure the story is accurate and up to date, and maintain the interest and focus of those listening to the story. We also realize that whales are capable of speaking for themselves, and it is often necessary to watch in respectful awe as the whale tells its own story. The beauty of the humpback whale is that it can tell its story so capably—when a humpback whale breaches, everybody speaks the same language.

Watching whales is exciting and continually leads to a single central question, why do whales do that? When interpreting the significance of a given behavioral display, it is important to bear three considerations in mind: First, one must be cautious not to generalize across species, especially when the degree of evolutionary relatedness is as unclear as it is, for example, between the toothed and the baleen whales. Second, given the high energy and degree of complexity of many humpback behaviors, one must recognize the possibility that the behaviors likely

High energy behaviors are expensive to produce, and may serve a variety of functions.

serve a variety of functions. The particular "meaning" of a behavioral display must be cast in terms of the context in which it occurs, and one must be prepared to reinterpret the behavior as the context changes.

The third caveat to be considered is that behaviors may be interpreted at a variety of levels. That is, we may ask why a whale breaches from the viewpoint of how that behavior evolved from an earlier, related species, or we might wonder how the behavior allows the species to deal more effectively with the pressures of its current environment. Evolution and adaptation have been the "ultimate" causal explanations traditionally sought by biologists and ethologists interested in establishing the effect of environmental pressures on behavioral development across the millennia of evolutionary change.

The significance of a behavior from the "proximate" point of view is also important. In the life of a given animal, we might ask how a behavior develops ontogenetically, that is, how and when the behavior appears as an individual animal grows up. With a much more direct explanation in mind, we might even ask what immediate environmental incident triggered a given response. These proximate explanations have been most often sought by comparative psychologists interested in understanding behavior in the context of its flexibility and dependence on learning. Today's scientists interested in the general field of animal behavior attempt to qualify their hypotheses about behavior by setting them in the context of the type of explanation they are hoping to achieve.

The behaviors we describe have been observed during many hundreds of hours of observations in our own research activities, and have been reported in the scientific literature of other researchers. We have observed all of these behaviors either

When a humpback whale breaches, everybody speaks the same language!

from shore stations, from aircraft, from boats, or from underwater.

Not all behaviors occur with equal frequency, nor are they produced by all segments of the population. The aggressive displays appear most frequently among competing males. Calves exhibit most, but not all of the behaviors described. We often see calves engaging in what appear to be imitative behaviors, and we have observed many immature attempts to replicate adult forms of behaviors such as tail slaps and spy hops. While it is appropriate to refer to many of the calf activities as "play" behavior, it should be borne in mind that play is not just random activity, but practice of those behaviors that will become more important as the calf matures.

While many of the behaviors can be seen easily from the deck of a whalewatching boat, many may only see underwater behaviors documented in photographs or on film. It is not to be expected every time a whale is seen from a boat that it will immediately put on a display of spectacular behaviors; often you

Since whales will not always engage in exciting displays, whalewatching requires patience.

will see nothing more than an occasional blow. It takes a great deal of time, energy, and patience to see the wide range of behaviors that we have described.

In the remainder of this chapter we will describe the general contexts in which the behaviors defined in Chapter 17, A Guide to Behaviors, may be seen to occur. While the described behaviors can be clearly defined as discrete units, in reality they occur as parts of sequences in which important functions are met.

Humpbacks are unique in the wide variety of behaviors and displays they show above the surface.

Single behaviors seldom stand on their own and take on added meaning when considered as part of more extended interactions between whales or between the whale and its environment. Most important, it can be seen that categories of behaviors have developed during the process of evolution as graded means of communicating needs and intentions to other members of the species. Thus the various head behaviors can be roughly categorized in at least two ways: visual scanning and aggressive display. Similarly, respiration behaviors, when considered as a group, also demonstrate the potential for graded elaboration of behavioral states. Tail, pectoral fin, and breach displays offer the whale alternative ways to make its presence and perhaps intentions clear to others.

It should be noted that many of the behaviors we describe are those that have been most obvious to us because they occur above the water's surface. Such behaviors constitute only a portion of the whale's activity. In fact, since it is unclear how much of the above-surface behaviors are even perceived by other whales, their overall significance remains in question. One could argue that all surface behaviors are simply different ways to make noise. We think that this is highly unlikely, since the various behaviors do consistently occur in specific contexts. A more plausible argument is that surface behaviors simply reflect the endpoints of underwater activities that have greater significance for the animal. To the degree that this is true, however, one must recognize that changes in surface behaviors are at least correlated with changes in underwater behaviors. Given this perspective we now describe in rather broad terms the contexts in which various behaviors, visible from the surface, occur.

Many of the head displays that we see appear to serve an orientation or scanning

Tail, pectoral fin and head displays may be used to signal location or to communicate more complex behavioral states such as competition or aggression.

function or both. On those occasions where the head is brought above the surface of the water with the mouth deflated and often with the eye exposed, there is good reason to believe the whale may be visually scanning the surface of the water. Behaviors such as spy hops and head rises have been observed in a variety of cetacean species, including orcas, bottlenose dolphins, right whales, and gray whales. While we typically think of marine mammals as marvelously adapted

for an underwater existence, their ability to investigate what is above the surface is both well developed and amazing to observe.

A few years ago we were three miles off west Maui in our research boat with three student interns. While we were floating quietly during our lunch break with the engine turned off, a large female humpback suddenly surfaced beside the boat and blew. She then dove effortlessly below the boat, and when she surfaced on the other side, her head slowly emerged from the water directly beside us. We sat in stunned silence as she rose higher and higher until the tip of her head was more than fifteen feet above us. Her eyes just barely cleared the surface. She rotated slightly so that one eye appeared pointed directly at us. She held that position for a brief period and then silently slipped below the surface. It seemed her investigation had come to an end. As we peered over the side of the boat hoping to get a last glimpse of her below the surface, we heard the sound of dripping water behind us. We turned and once again saw her head towering above us at the other side, one eye intently peering into our boat. For the following one and a half hours, the huge whale passed back and forth under our boat, rising time after time until the tip of her head was high above ours, and close enough that each of us had the chance to reach out and touch her ventral pleats. Never have we seen the eye of a whale so closely, and it was difficult not to wonder what she may have been thinking as she intently studied those who were studying her.

Head displays also seem to be important in competitive encounters. Humpback whales have a wide repertoire of behaviors that can be used to signal aggression. The sight of one humpback coming headfirst out of the water and hurling itself down onto the back of

Head rises frequently occur in close proximity to boats, and may allow whales to visually scan the hull or even the people onboard.

another leaves little doubt as to the nature of the interaction. Not all aggressive behavior is so obvious. Displays vary along a continuum of intensity signaling increasing levels of aggression. Low-level displays include throat distension and head shaking; jaw claps and inflated head lunges are medium-level displays; and head slaps and head butts are more aggressive activities. Like many other species, a humpback appears to be able to warn intruding whales, or perhaps bluff them into thinking that it is bigger and more dominant than they are. For example, in distending the throat grooves by filling the mouth with water or air, the whale's apparent size increases considerably. If that doesn't work, then there are techniques for feigning attack. Finally, should all else fail, the head or other parts of the body can be employed as full-fledged weapons to drive the intruder away.

Aggressive displays may also involve a variety of respiratory behaviors. Underwater blows and bubble blasts are both noisy and highly visible, at least within a whale-

By inflating its mouth as it rapidly surfaces to blow, a whale can enhance its apparent size and generate increased visual and acoustic disturbances.

length or two of the animal carrying out the behavior. These exhalations may result from a kind of hyperventilation on the whale's part, or allow the whale to breathe more quickly and resume its underwater activities. At the same time, however, underwater blows and bubble blasts provide considerable information on the location, activity, and general state of the whale exhibiting the behavior.

Aggressive males may sometimes butt each other with their heads, leading to cuts and bloody scars.

Whales can create signals of aggression by blowing forcefully as they surface.

The creation of bubble trails and bubble screens is a frequent activity among groups of whales competing to get close to a female. We have seen from aerial observations that the bubble trail is most often laid by one of the lead whales, and therefore highly visible to any following animal. Bubble screens may be an attempt to mask or obscure the location of the bubbler. Bubble screens are even created in the vicinity of small boats and divers. Bubble trails, on the other hand, may serve a more direct communicative function such as signaling anger or distress.

At the surface an underwater blow or bubble trail is visible only after the whale has already moved several body-lengths away. The light turquoise blue of the rising bubbles is often mistaken for the whale itself. As a general rule the whale may be 150 feet or more away from where the bubbles surface. Of course there is an exception to every rule. We were once following a surface-active group of nine whales near the island of Kaho'olawe.

One animal in the lead repeatedly emitted underwater blows. Every time the bubbles surfaced, the whale appeared shortly afterward three to four body-lengths away. At one point an underwater blow erupted very near the boat. Feeling certain the whale was some distance away, one of us aimed and focused the camera in preparation for a nice fluke shot. But the whale changed its tactics and suddenly erupted through its own underwater blow,

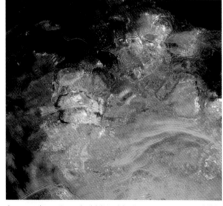

An underwater bubble blast causes a visible disturbance at the surface.

The whale's tail is not only the primary means of propulsion, but also serves as a formidable weapon.

head lunging directly in front of our boat toward one of the other whales nearby. It almost took the camera with it.

Another series of aggressive behaviors involves the tail, the powerful fifteen-foot-wide flukes that serve as the whale's primary mechanism of propulsion. Whalers and scientists interested in whale behavior have long been aware of the power of the fluke and its potential for aggressive use. Many exciting scrimshaw scenes of the hunt for sperm whales illustrate the hapless consequence of finding one's boat within range of the flailing flukes of a wounded whale. The gray whale earned itself the name of "devilfish" among whalers due to its ferocity when harpooned. Dolphins as well are quite capable of severely injuring conspecifics or unwanted intruders, such as sharks or even humans, with a slash of the flukes. Humpback whales have also been observed driving away orcas by lashing out with their flukes.

We have observed whales positioning themselves so as to present the posterior portion of their body toward an approaching whale, and sometimes toward an approaching boat. If the approaching object changes its direction to circle the whale, the animal will reposition itself to keep its tail pointed toward the intruder.

In doing so, it appears to have the flukes pointed straight down below the water, with the peduncle raised slightly above, but parallel to the water's surface.

Other fluke displays that appear to include an aggressive component are the tail slash and the tail slap. The tail slash looks like a karate chop with the fluke. The whale turns the posterior portion of its body toward a whale or intruder, and slashes its flukes back and forth while remaining in an upright position, usually with its head lower in the water than its flukes. The tail slap may be carried out in either an upright or inverted position. In either case, the whale positions itself with its pectoral fins stretched out to either side in order to prevent itself from rolling over, and then lifts its flukes above the water's surface. Often one can see half of the whale's body rising up out of the water. Once the flukes have reached the peak of their ascent, they are immediately brought flat down onto the water with a resounding and forceful slap that creates an explosion of whitewater. Most often the whale will tail slap repeatedly, a truly impressive sight. We have observed whales tail-slap more than one hundred times in a row, with slaps occurring as fast as we could count them. Tail-slap episodes such as these are

When approached closely underwater, whales may show apprehension by an unusual widening of the eye.

frequently initiated in the vicinity of other whales, approaching boats, and circling aircraft flying at low altitude. They are also observed when the tail slapper is alone.

Perhaps the most aggressive type of fluke display we have witnessed is one called the peduncle slap, or throw. The peduncle slap describes a behavior in which one whale hurls the rear half of its body up out of the water, and brings it down sideways against the water's surface or another whale. Our observations suggest that humpbacks tend to be either "righties" or "lefties" when engaging in behaviors like peduncle slaps. When we have seen the same individual peduncle-slap a number of times within an episode it has invariably favored one side or the other. We have also noticed that when animals do fluke-up dives, their tail may lean slightly to one side or the other, but always in the same direction in repeated dives.

Some of the described behaviors occur under circumstances that appear stressful, but are unrelated to clearly aggressive activity. One of these behaviors is what we have described as eye widening, a term we coined for lack of an already available one. We have seen photographs and film footage of humpback whales, especially of mothers and calves, in which the whale's eye is opened unusually wide. We have observed a similar reaction in captive dolphins that have been frightened by the introduction of a new and unfamiliar object into the water, or when taken out of the water while being transported to another location.

We believe that under certain circumstances humpback whales react with fear when approached underwater by humans. For example, it is not uncommon to find researchers or photographers who get impatient in their method of approaching whales and end up speeding in front of them in order to jump in the water and take photographs as the whales swim past the boat. Such a technique can

The humpback whale breach is a spectacular behavior for which there is no singular or simple explanation.

cause the whale considerable fright.

In conjunction with eye widening in humpbacks, we have noted the occurrence of bubbles streaming from the blowholes, sudden and intense beating of the flukes, and rapid diving. All of this leads us to conclude that eye widening and some forms of bubbling indicate fear, general stress, or both.

Undoubtedly the most exciting and spectacular humpback behavioral display is the breach. Forty tons of whale exploding from the ocean in the flurry of a twisting breach is a breathtaking sight. It is not entirely clear why whales breach. A variety of explanations have been proposed, for the behavior is seen in many cetaceans, odontocetes, and mysticetes alike. It has been suggested that humpbacks breach to signal to other whales that they are nearby; to stun fish while feeding; to knock off barnacles, lice, cookie-cutter sharks, or remoras; to signal behavioral states such as fear, stress, aggression, or playfulness; or simply to have a look at what is above the water's surface.

Many of these explanations seem unsatisfactory with respect to the hump-

During a breach, the whale's eye is exposed high above the surface for sufficient time to permit visual scanning over a wide distance.

back. They do not appear to feed while in Hawai'i, yet breaching occurs while the whales are here. Since humpbacks have been found with over one thousand pounds of barnacles attached to their bodies, breaching is apparently unsuccessful in dislodging such "hangers-on."

There is little evidence to indicate what kind of behavioral state might be indicated by a breach. Frequency of breaching decreases and aggression increases as the size of the pod increases. This suggests that breaching does not signal aggression within a pod, although it might be a means of warning other whales to keep away. One might wish to infer that breaching is a play activity, but it is unclear what constitutes "play" for a humpback whale, or how one might independently measure a state of playfulness. It may be that breaching occurs when whales are stressed or fearful. There is absolutely no basis for claiming that breaching is a sign of "happiness," in spite of the fact that observations of such activity led whalers to nickname the

humpback the "merry whale."

The possibility that whales may signal their presence by breaching is an interesting one. Certainly a breach alerts human observers not only to the whale's presence, but also to its exact location. Clearly a behavior as dramatic as a breach has the ability to serve as a form of communication. Acoustic analysis of sounds that emanate underwater from the reentry of a breaching whale is similar to the sound of a powerful oil-exploration air gun being detonated under the surface. There is little doubt that the acoustic signature of a breach is unique to that behavior and can transmit information on the fitness, the location, and perhaps the emotional state and even identity of the breacher. It is not unusual to see a single animal breach and within minutes a second, and sometimes even a third whale at some distance breach in apparent response. We have even seen these alternate breaches stretch into sequences of ten or twenty instances. Although we cannot be certain that the

©M&M/Sweet

When a forty ton animal crashes back to the ocean's surface, the underwater sound produced may communicate a number of features such as location, fitness or emotional state.

animals are breaching in response to each other, the consistency and timing of breach and response between the animals makes it difficult to avoid that conclusion.

A behavior as energy consuming as a breach is likely to serve a variety of functions. We believe that one purpose of the breach is to see what is above the water's surface. We have noted that in photographs of breaching whales, the orientation of the whale is in large part determined by the presence and location of the boat from which the photographer took the picture or other boats in the vicinity. Breaching whales often breach away from nearby boats, with the belly turned toward them. Such an orientation would generally put the boat in the whale's field of view and even provide stereoscopic (two-eyed) cues to enhance distance information. Other research findings about the frequency of breaches in the vicinity of boats, the effect of changes in boat direction or engine characteristics, and the number of times a given whale breaches suggest that whales visually scan the surface for boats they can hear but cannot visually or acoustically localize underwater. While breaching may

be a general startle response, the fact that the orientation of the whale is nonrandom with respect to the boat suggests that the whale is actually looking for or at the vessel.

Whatever the function or functions breaching may serve, it never ceases to amaze and amuse whalewatchers. People generally believe that in order to breach, the whale must dive deeply and propel itself above the surface of the ocean with many powerful beats of the tail. We actually have had the opportunity to observe whales breaching from an aircraft as well as while snorkeling. Surprisingly, a breaching whale starts within a body-length or two of the surface and only requires one or two beats of the tail to clear the water's surface. We have seen males, females, adults, juveniles, and even tiny calves engage in breaching behavior. Despite the incredible energy it must require, we have frequently observed whales breaching in excess of fifty times in a row. While we think it is amazing to see a calf jumping over and over again, it is anybody's guess how the poor mom can produce the milk required to sustain that kind of energy. If you need to be convinced of the kind of energy and coordination it takes to execute even a lazy breach, next time you are at the pool or beach, try jumping out of the water without pushing off the bottom.

Every breach is unique, but our favorite is what we call "the full breach with twisting kick," a display most common with subadults. After jumping almost clear of the surface, they seem to kick the tail sideways to complete the exit, and for a brief, yet spectacular moment, completely leave the ocean. When properly executed, the whale's body is completely clear of, and parallel to, the water.

It is virtually impossible to predict a breach. We are often asked whether breaches are more likely to occur in the daytime or the nighttime, in windy days or fine days, on sunny days or cloudy days, or on Mondays or Sundays. There is little correlation between any of these factors and the likelihood of a whale breaching. Frankly, we think the best predictor that a whale is going to breach is that we have just put our camera away.

The broad categories of mating and rearing offspring are important determinants of the behaviors of humpback whales in Hawai'i. These activities occur within an intricate web of social interactions permeating all facets of the whales' lives and activities while in Hawai'i. The temporal and geographical patterns of whale movement, the nature and length of social relations formed, and the behaviors in which the whales engage are all products of the need to mate, calve, and rear offspring. The pursuit of these needs is shaped within patterns of socialization that begin to affect the behavior of newly born calves from their first days in Hawai'i.

In the next section we review characteristics of migration, distribution, pod composition, and social interaction that are in large part determined by the complex rules, both biological and social, of reproduction and rearing in humpback whales.

It takes a tremendous amount of energy and coordination for such a huge animal to hurl itself completely above the ocean surface.

Chapter 19

WHERE HUMPBACKS ROAM

Humpbacks are found in all oceans of the world and engage in the longest-known migration of any mammal. Individual whales have been photographically identified in wintering and summering areas nearly three thousand miles apart, requiring an annual straight-line return journey of six thousand miles. They migrate long distances from polar waters near ice zones—rarely do they venture into the packed ice—to tropical winter breeding grounds near islands and banks. While widely distributed throughout all oceans, they aggregate in breeding waters of approximately 75°F (25°C). They prefer quiet bays and leeward sides of exposed reefs and large banks in waters of six hundred feet (one hundred fathoms) or less. One exception to the general pattern of migratory movement between polar feeding and tropical breeding areas is a relic population of whales found along the coast of Oman in the northern reaches of the Arabian Sea. While very little is known about the number of these animals or their overall movement patterns, it is believed these whales stay in the area throughout the year. The seasonal occurrence of monsoons drives sufficient prey into the area to release them from the need to migrate to polar feeding waters.

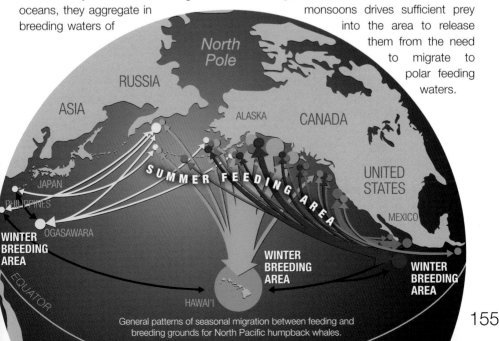

General patterns of seasonal migration between feeding and breeding grounds for North Pacific humpback whales.

North Pacific humpback whales feed in nearshore waters along the west coast of North America, through the Aleutian Islands, north and west into the Bering and Chukchi Seas, and down into the sea of Okhotsk and off the coast of northern Japan. In winter they migrate to three relatively discrete areas: in the western North Pacific from Japan to the Philippines, in the central Pacific around the Hawaiian Islands, and in the eastern North Pacific off the coasts of Mexico and Central America. Interestingly, a recent Pacific-wide analysis of resighting patterns indicates there is a yet undiscovered winter breeding site somewhere between Asia and Hawai'i.

The fact that humpbacks swim south in October and north in May in both hemispheres limits the opportunity for the Northern and Southern Hemisphere populations to intermingle. Even where both populations use the same equatorial waters off Costa Rica, they are not there at the same time. Under current climatic conditions, the equatorial isobath forms a real biological barrier.

The Hawaiian breeding stock comprises 60 percent of the humpback whales in the North Pacific. The summer feeding locations of the Hawaiian humpbacks stretch from southern British Columbia in the east to the Bering Sea in the west. Four predominate feeding areas, stretching north-northwest in a band from southeastern Alaska, to Yakutat Bay, Prince William Sound, and the western Gulf of Alaska, have also been identified. Research suggests that humpbacks mix on the breeding grounds in Hawai'i, but segregate into separate summer feeding areas. The majority of whales spend June through September feeding on small fish and euphausiids. There is no reliable evidence that indicates humpbacks feed in Hawai'i. In the Southern Hemisphere whalers working off east Australia at

Moreton Island (latitude 26° south) reported that some of the southbound whales returning to their feeding grounds had food in their stomachs. Our work in Eden, off the southeast tip of Australia, has provided ample opportunity to observe humpback whales feeding late in their southward migration. While we have occasionally received reports of whales apparently feeding during the breeding season, Eden is unique in the number of animals, the density of available prey, and the extent of feeding behaviors occurring outside of polar feeding areas.

Why do whales migrate? As described earlier we can consider this question from both the ultimate and proximate perspectives. With respect to the evolution of migratory behaviors as an adaptive response, the two primary hypotheses that have been suggested are avoidance of predation and thermoregulation. Based on scarring patterns on whales in the Southern Hemisphere, scientists there argued migration was an adaptive response to the presence of high levels of orca attacks on juveniles. A recent test of the hypothesis based on data from the Northern and Southern Hemispheres, however, disputes that conclusion. A more cogent explanation for migration appears to be the need to ensure thermoregulatory balance for newborn calves. An analysis of worldwide habitat for wintering populations (when calves are born) shows a very clear preference for surface-water temperatures in the range of 70°F to 75°F. Twenty years of observation have demonstrated, with few exceptions, that mothers with calves do not show up in Hervey Bay, Australia, until the water temperature hits 70°F.

With regard to the proximal triggers to migratory behavior, several hypotheses have been proposed. These include decreases in water temperature, daylight, and food supply, and increases in hormonal

We do not know the specific factors that control the timing of migratory movement between the feeding and breeding areas.

levels associated with reproductive activity. No single factor has been found solely responsible for migratory movement, and it is more than likely dependent upon a combination of factors. We must also realize that the immediate triggers for migration may be a function of gender and developmental stage. What causes a pregnant female to head out to Hawai'i may be different than what causes her to migrate in a resting year. In fact researchers in Alaska report whales there in every month of the year, and it may well be that in some years adult females don't migrate at all. Data from the breeding grounds in both Hawai'i and Australia suggest mature males may outnumber mature females nearly two to one during the winter season. The factors that determine when a sexually mature male sets out for Hawai'i are in all likelihood different from those that influence juvenile whales. Yearling animals, for the most part, have not yet been fully weaned and are likely to "follow the nipple"—where mom goes, they follow.

Since historically it has been not just difficult but impossible to follow the same whale from its breeding to its feeding grounds, figuring out how fast animals swim during migration has been a particularly intractable problem. From the days of early whaling, people knew that humpbacks could attain speeds of twenty miles per hour. No one really assumed, however, that they could travel that rapidly across such vast distances. It wasn't until the 1950s and 1960s that data collected from discovery tags and aerial surveys indicated that migrating whales traveled at an average speed of three miles per hour. Photographic resights of animals in both the Northern and Southern Hemispheres provide similar estimates of speed. More recently acoustic tracking of humpback whales along the east coast of Australia reported that nonsinging whales traveled at an average speed of two and a half miles per hour. The best available data, however, are coming from satellite tags, which have the advantage of being able to provide both short-term and long-term estimates of movements as well as being able to track animals over thousands of miles. Whales tracked by satellite in the South Atlantic covered two thousand miles at an average speed of two miles per hour. In Hawai'i, however, a mother and calf were documented traveling four hundred miles at nearly four miles per hour. All in all it is probably safe to estimate that migratory rates of humpback whales are in the range of two to four miles per hour. Of course whales moving over such extensive distances do not travel at a steady, continuous rate. They stop, backtrack, speed up, slow down, and take detours. When traveling from the feeding ground to the breeding ground, a whale's motivational state will be very different than during the return. Consequently, the rate of travel in the two directions may also differ.

The migration of whales between the feeding and breeding grounds is far from a coordinated, consistent pattern of movement. Whales seem to be constantly on the move in both directions. There does, however, appear to be a clear influence of gender and age on the pattern of movement. On the basis of data collected at shore-based whaling stations in Australia during the 1950s and 1960s, zoologists Graham Chittleborough and William Dawbin first suggested whales of different ages and sex arrive on the wintering grounds at different times. First to arrive are last year's mothers with their yearling calves, and subadult whales of both sexes. Next to arrive are the mature males and females. Females in late pregnancy arrive last. Pregnant females may remain longer on the feeding grounds since they need to store as much food energy as possible—not only for the journey to the breeding grounds, but to help them survive the trauma of birth, nursing, and rearing of their young all the way through their return migration. Individuals within the different groups arrive throughout the season, one category intermingled with the next. Peak numbers of each category occur within about a week of each other.

Mature females head northward from the winter breeding grounds as soon as they become pregnant, which puts some of them in the vanguard of the returning animals. Once they have become impregnated there is no need for them to remain in the breeding area, but there is considerable pressure to return to the feeding grounds to meet the energy

During migration, humpback whales maintain average speeds of between two and four miles per hour.

demands of pregnancy, parturition, and lactation during the coming two years. Also departing early are immature whales of both sexes. They are not part of the breeding population and are still growing and developing and need to regain access to feeding grounds. Mature males, in order to maximize their opportunities to mate, stay as long as there are mature females. On average it appears that an individual mature male will spend more time in the breeding grounds than a mature female. Mothers with newborn calves (who were among the last to arrive at the wintering area) generally leave last, to allow their calves time to develop a thicker layer of blubber for protection against the cold feeding waters they will soon be visiting for the first time. This pattern of arrival and dispersal allows humpbacks reproductive success and maximum feeding benefit from peak food resources in polar waters in the summer.

Whales may use a variety of navigation aids such as wind, current, salinity, and temperature patterns to move across vast ocean distances.

The ability to make this long and complex migration each year demonstrates an impressive capacity for pelagic navigation. Locating the isolated volcanic islands of Hawai'i each winter and returning to the feeding regions each summer requires the use of a variety of environmental clues and sensory capabilities. In addition to acoustic orientation and sensitivity to water and temperature currents, some studies suggest that navigation may depend upon a system designed to detect changes in the earth's magnetic field. Humpbacks may home in on their breeding and feeding grounds with the help of a metalloid substance, biomagnetite, found near the frontal lobe of their brains. Evidence from strandings indicates that beached whales that appear outwardly healthy may suffer from disorientation due to electrical storms high in the atmosphere, which create distortions in the earth's magnetic field. Subsequent experimental research has called these conclusions into question.

Whatever their secret of pathfinding, humpbacks regularly appear in Hawaiian waters in mid-October. The whales do not arrive en masse but flow in and out of the islands from October through May, although stragglers do arrive as late as July.

While in Hawai'i, whales of both genders and of all ages move widely throughout the islands, making it difficult to accurately determine the residency time of any specific individual. Animals seen in a given location on one day are unlikely to be there the next—"Here today, gone to Maui." Animals seen off Maui at one point in the season may later be seen off Kaua'i or Hawai'i Island, and they may subsequently return to Maui before departing for the feeding ground. Based on analysis of photographs, it has been determined that 90 percent of the whales spend less than four weeks in Hawai'i. The animals identified with the longest residency periods (two months or more) appear to be males. This suggests that males try to arrive early and stay late to maximize their ability to find receptive females.

Chapter 20
FAMILY, FRIENDS, AND RIVALS

Affiliations between animals while in Hawai'i are highly variable and generally of short duration.

Humpbacks do not appear to form stable groups in Hawai'i, with the exception of the mother and calf. We do find a variety of pod types, but just because animals temporarily associate as one group does not mean interaction may not be taking place between that group and another whale or group of whales at some distance. We simply do not know what the effective range of communication for humpback whales is. In any case, it is apparent from both boat and shore-based observations that interchange occurs frequently between the various pods of whales that are seen moving about the islands.

Nearly 90 percent of the pods observed in Hawai'i are comprised of one, two, or three whales. The remaining groups tend to range from four to eight whales. On rare occasions, however, we have encountered pods of more than twenty whales and heard reports of groups of even sixty animals. Perhaps as the number of animals migrating to Hawai'i increases, such large groups may be seen more frequently. The size of the pod seems to depend upon the activities in which the whales are engaged, such as weaning, courting, mating, fighting, nursing, singing, resting, playing, or just plain swimming.

Single whales are generally considered to be males, an idea originally based on the findings of Japanese whaling data. Pods of two whales may include two adults, two subadults, an adult and subadult, a mother and yearling, or a mother and calf. The frequency of two-whale pods decreases across the season. If pregnant females tend to travel in the company of another whale, it may suggest that humpbacks form larger aggregations prior to leaving the islands for Alaska. With the exception of the mother-calf pair, pods of two whales do not appear to be characterized by any unique behavior patterns, except that they tend to be rather boring animals to watch. It has been shown that the relative frequency and variety of behaviors increase as pod size increases.

Large pods of whales generally engage in a variety of aggressive activities believed to be associated with competition for mates. These pods are seen infrequently and remain together for only brief periods of time. Often they contain a calf and sometimes one or more subadult whales. Perhaps because of the high percentage of conspicuous activities found in these large pods, they are often found accompanied by a variety of other cetaceans. These

have included bottlenose, spinner, spotted, and rough-toothed dolphins, false killer and pilot whales, and even on one occasion a northern right whale and, on another, a fin whale.

Pod composition is constantly changing, with animals moving from group to group. Affiliations between animals may be as brief as ten to fifteen minutes and seldom last more than a few hours. In large pods the arrival and departure of animals is usually accompanied by many high-energy displays. The change in smaller pods may be more subtle. We recall one particular group we spent the better part of six hours following and photographing. Although there were never more than eight animals in the pod at any one time, when we analyzed the images for individual identification, we discovered twenty-six unique flukes. On the basis of acoustic recordings, it appears that pods remain socially active all throughout the day and night. Even in the middle of the night it is possible to hear whales breaching, pec-slapping, and tail-slapping just offshore. In fact, full-moon whalewatches have recently become a popular activity on Maui.

Whales continue to engage in acoustic communication and high energy behaviors around the clock, with some evidence suggesting that they are even more active at night.

Chapter 21
GIVING BIRTH

Humpback calves are both conceived and born in the vicinity of the Hawaiian islands. Data collected by biologists working aboard whaling ships revealed that ovulation in females, and increased testis weight and spermatogenesis count in males, peak during the winter months. It has also been found that the gestation period for humpbacks is ten to twelve months. Newborn calves are frequently seen in early December, and are quite common by the end of January. The rather surprising fact, however, is that there is little firsthand evidence of actual births in Hawaiian waters. On one occasion we watched a large female for approximately two hours sitting almost stationary at the surface, slowly undulating her tail flukes and caudal peduncle. Within an hour and a half of our first observations, we noticed a tiny calf appear alongside her and then swim to the tip of her head. We also observed a tiny

While it is clear that calves are born in and around the Islands of Hawai'i, direct observation of a birth in the Islands has never been documented.

At birth the calf must be highly mobile and capable of learning new behaviors by imitating its mother.

calf sitting quietly over its mother's head during an aerial survey off the island of Moloka'i several years ago. Approximately six hours later we found them nearly in the same location. The mother was still lying almost motionless at the surface while the calf rested quietly by her head. We thought at the time that the first incident involved a birth, and in the second observation, we think we saw a new mother and calf within a few hours of birth. The most compelling evidence to date of a birth in Hawai'i was the recovery of placental material just offshore of Lahaina, which was later determined to have the same biochemical composition as humpback whale placenta. No one has yet provided clear evidence of an actual humpback whale birth in these waters.

The only well-documented occurrence of a humpback whale birth, to our knowledge, occurred recently off the coast of Ecuador. A whalewatching boat operating from Puerto Lopez, a small fishing village near the central coast, came upon a single animal lying at the surface. Both video tapes and photographs show the animal breathing frequently, staying at the surface, and slowly moving the rear half of its body back and forth in the water. The whale then submerged and stayed down for fifteen minutes. Suddenly the area where the whale submerged turned blood red, and only a few seconds later the whale popped to the surface with a tiny calf by her head. The light colored calf's dorsal fin was doubled over. The mother slowly moved her tail rhythmically through the water, and soon thereafter a large placenta came to the surface. Over the next five minutes the mother gently nudged the calf to the surface and after a brief period of time they slowly swam farther to sea. The placenta was brought onboard the whalewatching boat where it was photographed. Too large to easily bring back to shore in the small, twenty-foot vessel, the placenta was left behind once it was photographed.

The captain of a whalewatch boat in Ecuador retrieves a placenta from the water after witnessing the birth of a calf.

Newborn calves can generally be identified by their light coloration and the relatively small mouth area, compared with adults.

While many claim to have witnessed a birth, it is found on closer examination that the observer only *thought* they saw a newly born calf. The reality however, is that in the absence of a well-documented, firsthand observation, it is difficult to confirm that a birth has occurred.

It is possible that many calves are born while the mothers are still en route to Hawai'i, although we have seen a number of obviously pregnant whales from both the air and underwater. It may also be that births generally occur at night. Whatever the timing, a humpback whale mother in late pregnancy selects an area where she and her newborn offspring will be free from harassment by preying sharks, sexually active males, and unpredictable boats. Newborn calves are almost white in color and begin to darken within hours of birth. Close examination will also show that the dorsal fin is doubled over nearly flat against the back, and fetal folds along both sides of the body. We have observed such calves on a number of occasions.

Following a period of perhaps a week, during which the mother and calf remain in nearshore waters, they extend their range of travel to include deeper water, within two to three miles offshore. As they do so, they frequently either join, or are joined by a third whale. This escort whale is generally assumed to be a sexually active male, but is not the calf's father. The escort whale does not remain with the mother and calf for more than a day at most, with most associations lasting for only a couple of hours, or in many cases, only a few minutes.

Frequently the escort whale will leave the mother and calf if a boat approaches, while on other occasions, it will carry out defensive maneuvers such as positioning itself between the mother and calf and approaching boat. When there are divers in the water, the escort may also interpose itself, or create a visual screen by blowing bubbles out of its blowholes. The escort may even threaten a boat or diver with its flukes. Once while we were swimming next to and photographing a mother and calf, an escort whale suddenly appeared sixty feet below, heading directly toward us at high speed. We knew that escorts often

Mothers with young calves often attract multiple male suitors, despite the fact that lactating females seldom ovulate.

interpose themselves between the mother-calf pair and intruding whales, boats, or divers. Since it was not readily apparent, however, how forty tons of escort was going to fit within the fifteen feet of space between us and the mother and calf, we held our breath and waited for what was quickly shaping up to be our last encounter with a humpback whale! To our relief and surprise the escort stopped about twenty feet below us, turned slightly on its side to expose one ominously bulging eye, and began blowing a stream of bubbles. As the bubbles rose to the surface, they struck our body and swim fins and immediately changed into a fine screen of smaller bubbles that completely enshrouded us, blocking our vision. When we regained our badly fractured composure and swam out of the bubble screen, the mother, calf, and escort were nowhere to be seen!

When a mother and calf are joined by a large number of other whales, there is generally a considerable increase in the amount and intensity of above-surface activity associated with highly aggressive attempts by the new arrivals to keep each other away from the mother and calf. It is now generally accepted that these groups of three to six or more whales chasing after mothers and calves are comprised primarily of males, attempting to displace each other, remain with the mother, and perhaps win the opportunity to mate with her. Data collected from whaling ships indicated some small number of females (perhaps 1 percent or fewer) undergo postpartum ovulation. That is to say, even though lactating (producing milk), a few of the females are still able to be impregnated. Postpartum ovulation could increase the number of calves born in a heavily exploited population or enable the mother to replace a stillborn or defective calf by a second pregnancy. Given the fact that there may be twice as many

A newborn calf may consume over 100 gallons of milk a day during frequent but relatively brief bouts of nursing.

reproductively active males than females, it may be well worth a male's time to seek out and court females even when they are accompanied by a suckling calf.

At birth, the calf is what one might consider precocial, that is, fully able to move about on its own, with all senses alert and functional. Mothers appear to engage in a great deal of contact behavior, which may enhance bonding between the mother and calf and ensures that the calf stays nearby. Using her head and pectoral fins, the mother can be seen nudging, corralling, and coaxing her calf to stay close by as they move along.

The characteristic position for the calf is just above and to one side of the mother's head, back towards her pectoral fin when under way. In this fashion the calf is always able to maintain visual contact with its mother and may be able to take advantage of the slipstream created by the mother. During the first weeks following birth, it is important that the mother and calf establish a powerful bond. This enables the mother to recognize and remain close to her calf, and the calf to learn and attend to the mother's system of communicative contact and vocalization. We now know that as the newborn calf either rests at the surface above its mother or wanders around exploring its surroundings within a few body lengths of its mother, they are in frequent vocal contact. Recent work in Hawai'i has demonstrated that the calf has a small repertoire of brief vocalizations. While less documented, there is also evidence that the mother produces relatively-low-frequency sounds.

The calf must begin to nurse almost immediately after parturition. The mother has two nipples, located on either side of the vaginal slit on her ventral surface, between the "bellybutton" and the anus. The nipples are connected to the lobes of the mammary glands, which are long and oval shaped, and lie between the blubber and the abdomen. The mammary glands of a mature female humpback may be as large as seven feet long and two feet wide. During lactation, they increase from about two inches to nearly one foot in thickness. This causes the nipples to protrude through the expanded mammary slits. After finding the nipple, the calf takes it in its mouth, and curls its tongue around

The bond between a mother and her newborn calf is very strong, and she will keep her calf close by at all times.

it. Interestingly the calf does not so much suckle as receive the milk that is squirted under pressure into its mouth. Apparently the stimulation of the nipple by the calf results in a reflexive ejaculation of the milk by the mother.

Whales' milk is much more viscous, or thick, than the milk of terrestrial mammals. It has less water than the milk of other mammals (40 to 50 percent for the humpback versus 80 to 90 percent for many domestic animals), much more fat (40 to 50 percent as compared to 2 to 17 percent), and about twice the concentration of protein. Approximately 100 to 130 gallons of milk are produced per day. The highly-concentrated, prolific

quantities of milk permit the calf to grow at the rate of nearly a foot per month. The newborn humpback averages twelve to fourteen feet in length and weighs upwards of two tons, and will double its overall length within a year.

Because the mother provides her calf with such enormous quantities of food while apparently not feeding herself during the calf's first two to three months, the mother must recognize and feed only her own calf. It is also important that she not waste her resources on a calf that shows any indication of not being able to survive. In keeping with such expectations, it has been repeatedly observed that mothers with newborn calves do not affiliate during the first few weeks following parturition. In Hawai'i we have never observed more than one newborn calf in a pod. In Hervey Bay, Australia, we see mothers and calves en route from primary breeding areas in the north to southern feeding areas. The calves we see there are, for the most part, six or more weeks of age. As with many primate species and toothed whales and dolphins, mothers of older newborns are more tolerant of each other. In contrast to Hawai'i, where there never seems to be a pod with more than one calf, we have documented groups in Hervey Bay with as many as nine mother-calf pairs. These large groups can form during the return migration because it is less likely that calves will attempt to nurse from a female other than their own mother, and fewer reproductively active males are harassing them.

In Hawai'i mothers with calves are never observed together. During the southerly migration in Australia, however, we frequently see multiple mother and calf pods.

Nursing consists of frequent episodes of short duration, perhaps limited by the calf's ability to hold its breath and remain underwater. Lactation is believed to continue for eight to twelve months. Weaning begins in earnest during the mother's return to Hawaiian waters at the end of the calf's first year. During the calf's first summer with its mother in the colder, food-rich waters of the north, some ingestion of small fish or euphausiids may occur. Once a calf is weaned it has little contact with its mother.

We have frequently watched mothers and their calves as they search about for food in Alaska and near Eden, Australia. It

is an amusing sight to witness the antics of the calf as it accompanies its mother during her attempts to capture prey. More often than not it seems the calf creates such a disturbance that one wonders how the mother is able to feed at all. In Alaska we witnessed a large calf alternately reappear with either one of two adult whales within three hundred feet of each other at intervals of ten to fifteen minutes. It seemed one adult served as an occasional "baby-sitter" to allow the mother to feed successfully.

Infant mortality in humpback whales is relatively high. Between 25 to 30 percent of newborns will not make it beyond their first year. Some will die on the breeding grounds within a short period after birth. In the winter of 2008 we witnessed a newborn calf that floated ashore near Lahaina. It was still alive when it stranded, but died shortly after. Although there were sharks in the area, there was no evidence of mortal wounds on the animal. In the last thirty years there have been no more than fifteen to twenty stranded newborns in Hawai'i. But we have no idea what the relationship is between the number of stranded animals and those that die offshore and sink to the bottom. Because Hawai'i is essentially a small group of islands in the middle of the vast Pacific, we would anticipate only a very small percentage of dead calves would drift onto shore. There is of course no way of observing or documenting incidences of mortality on the way back to Alaska. But one would expect some calves would simply not have the endurance to last the entire way. Natural predators such as sharks and orcas, combined with ship strikes and entanglement in marine debris, add to the toll. For those that make it to the feeding areas, there is increased threat of these dangers.

While the bond between mother and calf is a strong, newborns do get separated. In Hawai'i we have seen a few

Nearly 30 percent of newborn calves will not survive their first year.

abandoned calves, which quickly become targets of predatory sharks. In Hervey Bay, Australia, we frequently observe older calves on their own wandering from pod to pod clearly in distress and separated from their mothers. These animals often appear in poor physical condition. It is not clear whether they have been abandoned or separated and lost. In any case a newborn calf separated from its mother is not going to survive. Adult females other than the mother will not adopt or nurse abandoned calves. On their own, it will be matter of time before they starve or become prey for marine predators.

The likelihood of being able to capture and rehabilitate an abandoned calf in an oceanarium or similar facility is virtually nil. We know so little about the factors associated with diet and parental care that the one attempt we know of to save an abandoned humpback calf ended rather quickly in its death from starvation. The reality is that abandoned calves, in most cases, are sickly and unable to survive even with their mother. It may well be that mothers are able to detect less fit offspring, and rather than waste substantial resources on a calf that won't survive, they simply cut their losses and leave the calf to its own demise. The more tragic cases involve otherwise healthy calves whose

mothers die either from natural causes or from human impacts. Despite their healthy state, they too face certain death without their mother.

Female humpback whales reach puberty at six to eight years in the North Pacific, but do not begin to have calves until they are almost twelve years old. Once they begin calving they undergo a cyclic pattern of giving birth, nursing, and then either resting or giving birth again. This would generally lead to a birthing interval of every two years. In some years, females appear to give birth immediately after having a calf the year before. This may be because they have ovulated following the loss of a calf, or they may ovulate and get pregnant even while nursing a calf. In other cases, perhaps related to age, but certainly depending upon overall physical conditions, females may go two or three years without a calf. It is not clear whether females continue to calve until they die or whether they experience a period of senescence in later years. The end result is North Pacific females have an average birth interval of twenty months (1.7 years). A variety of investigations indicate that the birthrate in Hawai'i is 7 to 8 percent per year.

Chapter 22
FINDING A MATE

Despite the indirect evidence that mating takes place in Hawai'i, we have yet to see unequivocal evidence of its occurrence. Since we know gestation ranges from ten to twelve months, the obvious implication is that mating must occur while the whales are in or near Hawai'i. Increased use of underwater cameras has led to a number of observations of what the whalers used to refer to as a "pink sea snake," the impressive four- to six-foot-long penis of the male. Nobody has yet witnessed an actual intromission. Our conclusions about courting and mating in humpback whales depend, in large part, on what we know about similar activities in other species of baleen whales, particularly the gray whale and the right whale. Such generalizations are used only to guide us in our observations of humpback whale reproductive behavior, since the mating systems of the different species of whales vary considerably.

Studies based on photographic identification and genetic analyses of skin samples confirm there are nearly twice as

Males outnumber females by nearly 2 to 1 on the breeding grounds, creating high levels of competition between the males for access to females in estrus.

Sexually mature males must display their fitness to females and out-compete other males in order to obtain the chance to mate.

many males as females on the breeding grounds. Roughly half the females are in late pregnancy, so the number of females available for mating is even smaller. Males must therefore engage in strategies that will increase their chance to mate at the expense of other males, while females must use strategies that will ensure they mate with the fittest males possible. Not all males are of equal fitness and may use different strategies depending upon their place in the male hierarchy and the general availability of females. It has also been argued that not all females are of equal fitness. Those that have given birth in the previous year may be less physically fit than females that have not given birth for two or more years. Females who have just given birth and are lactating have the least resources available, even though they may undergo postpartum ovulation. In general some females may be more attractive to the males than others. The end result is that throughout the winter there are a wide variety of scenarios consistent with the changing needs and opportunities available to both the males and females in the breeding area at any given time.

Females moving through the inshore waters of the islands are periodically accompanied by sexually mature males. It is not known whether the females selectively approach males to whom they are attracted (perhaps by the male's song), whether the males actively search for receptive females, or both. Males do not appear to search in groups for females, although observations of singers joined by other males do indicate that they sometimes affiliate with other groups of males accompanying a female.

Once a male finds a sexually receptive female, other males soon appear. The

It appears that if a male can remain close to a female through an extended series of encounters with other males, he may win the chance to mate with her.

Males will sometimes use their huge heads to ram other males in an attempt to drive them away from a female in estrus.

original male must now work hard to keep those other males away. It is customary to think of the large baleen whales like the humpback as huge but sedate "gentle giants" quietly roaming across the world's oceans. This image is reinforced by the brief view most of us have of humpbacks when we see small groups of two or three whales, or a mother and her calf. In actual fact, observations of large, surface-active groups of males competing for a female during the breeding season provide a very different picture of the humpback's temperament.

As the males compete to "escort" the female (thereby increasing the likelihood of a mating opportunity) a high-speed chase begins. One of the males asserts himself as the primary escort, and some or all of the others attempt to challenge him. Head slaps, inflated head rises, tail slaps, peduncle slaps, and head butting occur with high frequency and great vigor. The whale most successful in remaining near the female generally does so by carrying out a wide variety of strenuous activities primarily involving the head and tail. The primary escort may have to prove himself a number of times over a period of hours. The female sometimes leads the way, with all the interested males (and sometimes curious subadults) strung out behind.

Not all of the accompanying whales actively engage in aggressive behavior. Most of the competitive activity appears to focus on the primary escort, a secondary escort who is challenging him, and possibly one or two other aspiring escorts. These pods can sometimes build to fifteen, twenty, or even more animals. Whales are continually entering and leaving the pod, and minor skirmishes may break out among animals on the periphery. The major focus however remains on the female and the dominant males that surround her. The role of the female in competitive

When males detect the presence of a sexually active female, they will rush to join the pod and attempt to displace the primary escort.

pods is somewhat unclear. She may be running from the group of highly excited males because she wants nothing to do with them, or she may be providing them the opportunity to "show their stuff" as they chase her and fight with each other. Sometimes the female appears to show her approval of the primary escort by falling in close beside him while he leads the chase.

Following a period of jostling, bumping, charging, and countercharging, the fierce competition comes to an end. The primary escort is either displaced or maintains his position and the pod breaks. After the competition between males is complete, the female must somehow indicate her willingness to favor the attentions of the successful male. Whether actual mating occurs at that time or not is uncertain. Underwater observations of the competitive groups do show males with their penises extruded, but it is not clear whether this is a male competitive display or some form of enticement for the female to stay around.

At this stage the "courting pod" consists of the primary escort interacting with the female, sometimes in the presence of two or more spectator whales. The male and female engage in a great deal of body contact, including mutual pectoral fin caresses and slaps, belly-to-belly rubbing, alternate diving under one another, and a variety of forms of nuzzling with the head area. One whale may be seen engaging in a great deal of pec-slapping on the surface of the water, sometimes lying on one side while swimming slowly about with half of the tail exposed above the water, sometimes lying belly up, then rolling in the water while first one and then the other pectoral fin is raised high above the water and then brought splashing down onto the surface. The whale may lie belly up, raise both pectoral fins in the air, usually crossing them in the process, and then slap both simultaneously to each side. Pectoral fin displays such as these usually involve long bouts of repetitive slaps.

The relatively slow-paced swimming that usually accompanies these displays,

in conjunction with the almost total absence of threatening or aggressive tail behaviors, supports the conclusion that these are not the competitive, fierce bouts of jousting described earlier. On the other hand, if such activity were immediately preliminary to intromission, one would expect to see an erect penis somewhere in the courting pod, but none has appeared in the presence of such activity to date.

Following a period of intense competition, females may signal their interest in the primary escort with a series of pectoral fin slaps, as though applauding him for his performance.

The failure to see evidence of mating is particularly intriguing, given the rather immodest behavior of other species of mysticetes. Male right whales and gray whales may be seen rolling at the surface, waving their erect penises in the air during their courtship activities.

The role of spectators during the period when the primary escort and the female begin to attend to each other is not clear. They may remain in the vicinity as hopeful understudies should the female lose interest in the primary escort. They may simply be curious onlookers. Humpback whales mate promiscuously (both males and females mate repeatedly with different partners throughout the breeding season) and the members of the audience may be other males or females waiting for their own opportunity. In some baleen species, the additional whales may even help out during copulation by holding the partners in place.

It may well be the case that courtship is a very protracted business, extending over days, or possibly weeks, with many false starts. We have observed thousands of competitive encounters between humpback whales, and watched as males bloodied and bruised each other with gut-wrenching intensity. Typically discretion has always been the better part of valor and bested individuals simply leave the pod. Although ferocious, such encounters do not normally seem to be fights to the death. In 1996, however, our research team collected observations on a male humpback that lost its life in a competitive group. The whale had been reported by a whalewatching boat as a member of a surface-active group comprised of four animals. The group was engaged in highly aggressive interactions, including head butts, peduncle slaps, and underwater blows. Following two hours of competition, one whale surfaced without blowing, rolled on its side and remained motionless. The other animals immediately changed their behavior and began to swim around the now-dead whale, spy-hopping and caressing him with their pectoral fins. From the surface it looked like two of the animals

were caring for their fallen comrade, supporting him at the surface with their pectoral fins and caressing him with their heads. Underwater photographs clearly showed that in fact one of the whales, with an extruded penis, was holding the dead animal in its pectoral fins and was attempting to mate with it. While it is impossible to say exactly what killed the animal, our conclusion is that competitive groups can exact a significant toll, with the loser facing both a fatal and ignominious end.

Escort whales are frequently seen in the company of mothers and calves. They have always been found to be males. Perhaps the mother, slowed down as she is by the presence of her calf, is an attractive target for males. Mothers do not appear to always return an escort whale's interest. A possible indicator of the mother's degree of readiness to be attended by an escort may be the position of the calf during the period of time that the escort is present. Often the calf remains on the side of the mother opposite to the escort, with the escort trailing to the rear. On other occasions, the mother and escort will appear closer together than the mother and calf, and they can even be seen contacting each other with their pectoral fins, with one whale diving below the other while the calf remains close to the surface,

two or three whale-lengths from the adults. As mentioned previously, few lactating females are ovulating and such approaches would therefore be fruitless. On some occasions escorts may be inexperienced or less-dominant animals, either practicing or making desperate attempts to mate with the female. On other occasions, particularly late in the season when few receptive females remain, adult males may simply be engaged in last-ditch attempts to find an ovulating female. Analysis of the individual histories of females suggests that when escorts approach mothers and calves, either singly or in large competitive groups, the mothers are less-fit animals. More dominant animals are found competing for what may be viewed as more attractive, nonlactating, sexually receptive females.

When competition pods are approached by a boat, the primary or secondary escorts will often respond as though the boat is another approaching whale. We have observed interposition, bubble screens, tail threats, inflated head rises, and underwater blows when vessels approach competition pods. When there are three or more highly active escorts, boats are generally ignored if they remain at some distance. Boats that pursue the pod may create havoc. A variety of threats and defensive maneuvers may result, or the whales may disperse. Such encounters may actually interfere with the normal courtship dynamics and reduce the chances of successful mating. In general the less obtrusive the boat, the greater likelihood it will simply be ignored.

Even an innocent and innocuous boat making every reasonable attempt to stay out of the fray, however, might become part of an unexpected close encounter. Our whalewatching vessel, the *Ocean Spirit*, was once stopped in the water with one hundred passengers on board happily watching a large, competitive pod more than one hundred yards away. For unknown reasons the female came over and sat underneath the *Ocean Spirit*, while the remainder of the group continued to fight with each other. As the aggressive activity increased, the pod slowly got closer and closer to the whalewatching boat. At one point the primary escort head-butted a challenger, pushing him into the side of the vessel. In a desperate act to get close to the female, the primary escort swam underneath the boat and tried lifting it away from her. The stern of the vessel came six inches out of the water. While the passengers were somewhat apprehensive, they were nonetheless highly impressed with the persistence of the primary escort. Eventually the female moved off with her suitors close behind. Neither the boat nor any of the whales suffered any damage.

Section II

WHERE WHALES AND HUMANS MEET

Chapter 23

SAVING WHALES

The humpback whale has been formally listed as an endangered species in the United States. The legal framework for ensuring the recovery and protection of humpback whales is derived from the Endangered Species Act (ESA) and the Marine Mammal Protection Act (MMPA). In 1991 the National Oceanic and Atmospheric Administration (NOAA) published the *Final Recovery Plan for the Humpback Whale.*[1] Conservation actions for humpback whales have been largely guided by the objectives of this document: "(1) maintain and enhance habitat; (2) identify and reduce human-related mortality, injury and disturbance; (3) measure and monitor key population parameters to determine if recommended actions are successful; and (4) improve administration and coordination of the overall recovery effort for this species." National Marine Fisheries Service (NMFS), a branch of NOAA, is responsible for implementing terms of the recovery plan and enforcing other federal statutes related to humpback whales.

It would be misleading to discuss the depletion and recovery of humpback whales without first pointing out that most population estimates for marine mammals are only a best guess. Cetaceans in particular are extremely difficult to count because they spend a fair amount of time underwater. Humpbacks spend about 80 percent of their life below the surface! In addition, the great whales,

---

1   National Marine Fisheries Service. 1991. Recover Plan for the Humpback Whale (*Megaptera novaeangliae*). Prepared by the Humpback Whale Recover Team for the National Marine Fisheries Service, Silver Spring, Maryland, 105 pp. 33.

Three decades of research based on photographic identification of individual whales has helped show that in most areas of the world, humpback whales have been making a slow but steady recovery.

like the humpback, often travel alone or in small pods making them difficult to sight. They migrate over huge expanses of ocean along routes that are impossible to monitor. Population estimates then are derived from statistical models that depend upon photographic evidence, systematic surveys, modern and historical whaling data, satellite tags, acoustic monitoring, and genetic models. Statisticians have developed creative and insightful ways to reduce variability in the estimates, but variability nonetheless remains. Population estimates are typically given as a range of values with a 95 percent probability that the correct number falls somewhere within that range, which is often unsatisfactorily large. The range is also known as the "confidence interval"; the larger the confidence interval, the poorer the estimate. The current number of humpback whales worldwide is estimated by the International Whaling

Commission to be sixty-five thousand to eighty thousand animals. The North Pacific population numbers from seventeen thousand to twenty thousand humpbacks, with approximately 60 percent visiting Hawai'i each winter.

In order to determine whether or not the status of humpback whales is endangered, the current population has to be compared with the number of whales that would be present if they had not been hunted or otherwise eradicated by humans. We don't know exactly what that number was. We can only make estimates based on recorded catches of humpbacks. Historically whaling captains were fairly diligent about maintaining locations and number of whales killed. Based on available logbook records, scientists have reconstructed how large the population must have been to permit the kind of catches that were recorded, the rate at which those numbers changed from year to year, and the estimated number of whales alive now. Based on such estimates, by the 1980s it was believed that the prewhaling worldwide number of humpback whales was in the vicinity of two hundred thousand, with fifteen thousand in the North Pacific.

In 1966 the number of humpbacks in the North Pacific was estimated at fewer than six hundred. The International Whaling Commission instituted a ban on commercial hunting of humpback whales in the Northern Hemisphere. (The Southern Hemisphere stock has been protected from commercial whaling since 1963.) Scientists estimated the stock should recover to 60 percent of its prewhaling capacity within twenty years. By 1986 it was estimated there were fewer than fifteen hundred humpback whales in the North Pacific, and recovery seemed either nonexistent or incredibly slow. We now know one important reason for the slow recovery. Despite the ban on whaling, the Soviet whaling fleet continued to illegally kill humpback whales in relatively large numbers in both the North and South Pacific during the 1960s and 1970s.

Revelations of large numbers of Soviet takes has required a reassessment of the original stock and the number of animals required before recovery can be fully proclaimed. It is now believed there were approximately fifty thousand humpback whales in the North Pacific and five hundred thousand worldwide before whaling. Current estimates of humpback populations indicate they have only recovered to approximately 25 percent of their original numbers worldwide (although recovery in the North Pacific population may be closer to 50 percent). Humpbacks in the North Pacific will not be considered for delisting from endangered to threatened until they reach a sustained population that is at least 60 percent of its original size, which would be thirty thousand animals. At the current 7 percent rate of recovery, delisting could be considered within ten years.

Whether delisting ever does occur, however, does not simply depend upon a continued cessation on commercial whaling. The sad truth of the last twenty years is that even in the absence of commercial whaling, humpbacks continue to die in large numbers from other

Continued illegal whaling of humpbacks during the 1960's and 1970's greatly interfered with recovery of populations in both the Northern and Southern hemispheres.

Even in the absence of commercial whaling, marine species around the world are increasingly threatened by a wide variety of human activities.

irresponsible anthropogenic impacts. The threats continue to grow in number and intensity with each passing year. Even if whales continue to escape the harpoons of whaling ships, they must face the growing possibility of being struck by huge, fast-moving ships; of getting entangled and drowned in the ever-increasing drift nets and marine debris carelessly dumped into the ocean; of being poisoned from the toxins that run from our coastlines into the oceans; of becoming confused and even permanently damaged by various forms of human-induced noise; of having their food disappear because of overfishing and global warming; and of being displaced from their critical habitat by human action. Any animal must be able to adapt to changes in its environment to ensure their survival, but it is difficult for humpbacks and other marine mammals to adapt to changes that literally happen overnight. It remains to be seen whether we can control the size and activity of the human population to secure the continued existence of so many of the species with which we are meant to share this planet.

Worldwide populations of marine mammals face an increasingly complex array of anthropogenic (human-induced) assaults on not only their environment but also their very life. Beyond the threat of being hunted for food, for use in by-products, or for scientific research they now face death and degradation from fisheries' bycatch and entanglement; ship strikes; toxins that enter the marine ecosystem from runoff, acid rain, or direct dumping; oil spills; marine debris; noise pollution; displacement from their preferred habitat; and global climate change. Humpback whales also face these threats as they make their annual migration between Alaska and their birthplace in Hawai'i. Not all of these threats seem to be of equivalent importance in Hawai'i. Noise pollution, entanglement in fishing gear and marine debris, and ship strikes pose the greatest threats.

Despite the cessation of commercial whaling, so-called "scientific whaling" continues to provide meat that is sold in markets throughout the world.

Increasing numbers of whales are killed each year by ship strikes, pollution, entanglement in fishing gear, oil exploration and military exercises.

The sources of noise pollution in Hawaiian waters are numerous. They include the use of high-intensity underwater sounds by military-industrial organizations, large ships in military operations and commerce, smaller recreational and ocean tourism vessels, and underwater construction. The military use of low-frequency sonar as part of a number of experiments to monitor large areas of the ocean may pose the greatest threat. The general principal underlying these experiments is to broadcast very-low-frequency sounds at incredibly high amplitudes that will travel thousands of miles underwater or bounce off of objects deep in the ocean. By reading the sounds when they either get to their destinations or bounce back from objects they strike, it becomes possible to monitor with great sensitivity what is going on below the surface. Clearly this has important military

applications. Unfortunately, the sounds used also threaten species of marine life with concussive injury or interference with their normal patterns of underwater acoustic communication.

All vessels make noise. Lots of vessels make lots of noise, and as the ambient noise in the oceans increases, many species have to adjust their vocalization patterns to be heard above the racket. This has particular significance in Hawai'i, as the humpback whale song is vital for reproductive success and for the many social sounds made between mothers and calves. Increasing levels of nearshore boat traffic may alter the distribution patterns of humpback whales. While underwater construction can create significant disturbance as well, in most cases the work can be scheduled to take place when the whales are absent.

Fishing and cargo nets, lines, traps,

Whales are constantly under threat from boat strikes (top). Sometimes strikes result in relatively minor wounds (second photo from top), but all too often animals are severely wounded by such encounters (bottom two photos).

and pots from recreational and commercial fishing boats become deadly items when lost or abandoned in the marine environment. As they get caught up in currents and drift thousands of miles, pieces of gear become entangled and grow into huge ghost nets which trap marine animals, destroy coral reefs, and even trap divers and swimmers. In 1990 a huge area of marine debris was discovered stretching hundreds of miles from just northwest of Hawai'i across to Japan. It was recently estimated that the mass of trash contains one hundred million tons of human garbage, and its tendrils reach hundreds of meters below the surface. In 2004 a three-ton mass of fishing gear was found floating in Kāne'ohe Bay, O'ahu. For over ten years we led an effort to clean up marine debris from beaches on the uninhabited island of Kaho'olawe, near Maui. With the help of many volunteers, including the U.S. Navy, we removed up to ten tons a year. The masses of derelict fishing gear found in Hawai'i are not necessarily from boats operating within the islands. Because of prevailing winds and currents, gear from throughout the Pacific drifts towards the Hawaiian archipelago.

Only a small number of marine mammals have been found entangled in fishing gear in Hawai'i. Analysis of scarring patterns on humpback whales photographed in Hawai'i, however, indicates that approximately 30 percent of the animals show evidence of entanglement at some point in their migration between summer feeding and winter breeding sites. These estimates use photographs of tail flukes that almost certainly underrepresent the size of the problem. Some scars may heal and disappear, other scars may be missed because they are on other parts of the body, and the scars of many animals may never be seen at all because the weight of the gear dragged them to the bottom.

This whale has suffered a blunt trauma wound, probably from a strike from the bow of a large ship, and is unlikely to survive.

Collisions between whales and vessels are a growing problem worldwide. As the population of whales in Hawai'i has grown, so have interactions between whales and boats. These have ranged from curious whales bumping and lifting boats to collisions that have left clear evidence of injury. Interestingly, the relative number of boats has not changed significantly since the early 1990s, while the population of whales has nearly doubled. Our research has shown that for boats operating off of Maui during the peak of the whale season, one can expect an unanticipated surfacing of a whale within three hundred yards of the boat's heading once every nine miles traveling at an average speed of six miles per hour (five knots). Even with a team of two or three experienced observers, these surprise encounters will occur. Fortunately most of the boat-whale encounters in Hawai'i involve boats less than sixty-five feet in length, weighing less than forty tons, and the majority traveling under seventeen miles per hour (fifteen knots), variables that are not usually sufficient to cause much damage to either party.

When the mass of the boat is less than the mass of the whale, the whale may sustain injuries but the encounter is unlikely to be fatal. When the mass of a vessel is significantly greater than the whale it strikes (one hundred tons or more), the result is lethal 50 percent of the time at fourteen miles per hour (twelve knots), 80 percent of the time at seventeen miles per hour (fifteen knots) and 100 percent of the time at speeds of twenty-two miles per hour (nineteen knots) or faster. The recent introduction of a high-speed ferry between O'ahu and Maui, some 350 feet long, weighing nearly eight hundred tons (fully loaded), and capable of traveling at speeds in excess of forty-three miles per hour (thirty-seven knots) has raised grave concerns about the likelihood of striking and killing humpbacks. At that size and at any speed over eleven miles per hour (ten knots), a struck whale doesn't stand a chance. At the peak of the season there may now be as many as one thousand humpback whale calves throughout the islands. They are particularly sensitive to vessel strikes. How unfortunate if all of our efforts to keep them out of the sights of whaling ships only resulted in having them die from unintended vessel strikes.

Chapter 24
MAKING A DIFFERENCE

Whalewatching has become a big business in the United States. Millions of enthusiasts go whale-watching in America each year. The total revenue from all whale activities, including sales of memorabilia and memberships in whale organizations, amounts to hundreds of millions of dollars. When compared with killing whales, recreational whalewatching represents a low- or non-consumptive utilization of a remarkably renewable economic resource.

Since the protection of North Pacific humpback whales from commercial hunting in 1966 and the implementation of a worldwide moratorium on whaling in 1986, the concept of conservation and management must be examined in a new and different light. Past whale management strategies reflected consumptive needs, for example the determination of the maximum number of whales that could sustainably be removed from a given population. Early research was based on meeting these needs. The 1970s brought with it an outraged public that was hell-bent on saving the whales, fueled by spectacular underwater films and fascination with the humpbacks' curious song. They demanded more information, which was to be gained from living whales rather than dead. From

Responsible whalewatching represents a low-impact utilization of a remarkably renewable resource.

the beginning a most curious marriage was formed, with the scientists making new and exciting discoveries, and the public eagerly awaiting each new insight.

Whalewatching has become a spring-board for stimulating further interest in the whales, their habitat, and the value of "saving" them. For many, a whalewatching trip is their initial venture on the ocean, and provides the opportunity

Whalewatching is more economically viable than whale hunting. A whale can be watched a million times, but it can only be killed once.

to experience firsthand the dependence of whales on the marine environment and to understand how essential it is that the oceans be kept clean and uncongested. In the words of sociobiologist Stephanie Kaza: "The power of this experience should not be underestimated: through cetacean education there is an avenue for counteracting the tendency toward self-destruction that dominates world politics and human relationships today. With whales and dolphins, we begin to observe the natural order of life and validate our own experiences of that which we hold in common."

PACIFIC WHALE FOUNDATION

The Pacific Whale Foundation, a nonprofit marine research, education, and conservation organization, has helped promote marine mammal conservation through new legislation to regulate human activities, the development of protected areas, and heightened public awareness of the status of marine mammal populations. Throughout its existence the primary source of funding for its programs has come from whalewatching. All profits realized from these activities go directly to support the research, education, and conservation initiatives of the organization.

As leaders in the development of responsible whalewatching, Pacific Whale Foundation has been acutely aware of the ever-changing nature of the relationship between humans and marine mammals over the past three decades. There has been a rapid increase in venues promoting whale and dolphin watching excursions all over the world. Today more than ten million people a year venture out to see whales and other marine mammals in the wild. This has given rise to increased concerns about potential damage to vulnerable marine mammal populations. The need to take whatever steps possible to prevent damage to threatened and recovering species is recognized and appreciated. One response that has been taken in a number of areas around the world has to been to put regulations in place with a view to controlling human behavior in the presence of marine mammals. We generally support attempts to prevent some of the more egregious forms of harassment and disturbance that may cause harm. At the same time, we recognize that watching whales and dolphins is not the major threat they face—it is not even among the top five.

Resource managers the world over lament the fact that there is simply never enough funding to cover all the necessary bases. Regulating and patrolling whale- and dolphin-watching operations depletes resources better spent on trying to prevent the depredations of toxic runoff, noise pollution, fishery bycatch, ship strikes, depletion of prey species, habitat destruction, and global warming. The environment (and the species within it) is less threatened by whale- and dolphin-watching boats than by the daily activities of the ten million people who pay to go on the boats each year. Pacific Whale Foundation's philosophy is that reshaping the behavior of the ten million whalewatchers is of far more importance than regulating the activity of a few thousand operators. And its involvement in whalewatching over the past three decades has been driven by the belief that operators must accept a major share of the responsibility for reshaping that behavior.

The importance of educating visitors is certainly not a new concept. Much has been done in the interests of education in a wide variety of tourism settings. A failure to fully understand the interests and learning styles of the public, however, has limited the success of many marine wildlife viewing programs. We recognize the need to develop an "ecology of interpretation" that values and understands the convergence of unique elements in a whalewatching

episode: the operator, the whalewatcher, and the whale. And it is the operator who is in the best position to take the lead in planning how to reshape the behavior of the whalewatcher in the context of the journey to see the whale.

An effective education program requires an understanding of how learning occurs. Pacific Whale Foundation's marine conservation and education programs are based on three fundamental principles derived from learning theory:

1. Modeling is an effective way to shape desired behaviors in others.
2. Reinforcement increases the frequency of desired behaviors.
3. Opportunity to engage in desired behavior is a necessary part of the learning cycle.

Over time these three principles have been imbedded in all aspects in our development of operations, staff development, and guest services. We have undertaken a number of initiatives to enhance the educational and conservation impact of our programs.

Through responsible whalewatching we can educate millions of people a year to take better care of the environment.

Pacific Whale Foundation has been a leader in responsible whalewatching for three decades.

OPERATIONS:

Boat-based programs are operated on a daily basis by modeling the conservation behaviors we hope our passengers will emulate. Pacific Whale Foundation has developed a fleet of state-of-the-art, whale-friendly, environmentally sound vessels with purpose-built hulls; low-emission, high-performance engines fueled with blended biodiesel; protective devices around the propellers; and high-quality PA systems. An innovative solar- and wind-powered vessel is currently in the design stage, and it is slated to come online in the near future. Our "Whale Protection Devices" are the first of their kind for U.S. Coast Guard–certified passenger vessels, and we have prop guards on all our research and support vessels.

All vessels are fitted with low-flow toilets. The organization operates its own pump-out truck (powered by biodiesel), so no waste is discharged at sea. All plates, cups, utensils, and napkins are biodegradable and biocompostable.

They are fabricated from sugar cane, corn, and potatoes. Only seafood that has been harvested with sustainable techniques is served on board, and a Seafood Watch card is distributed to each passenger. All of our vessels carry reef-safe sunscreen, which is supplied free to our passengers. This reduces the amount of nonbiodegradeable sunscreen sloughing off snorklers' skin and damaging coral reefs.

Education is a critical component of ensuring marine tourism is part of the solution rather than part of the problem.

STAFF DEVELOPMENT:

It is of high importance that the captains, crew members, and naturalists view the vessels as floating classrooms where guests can be inspired to protect the environment and its species. Employee efforts to improve their own knowledge and engage in environmentally sound behaviors must be appropriately reinforced. All staff members are required to attend a variety of regularly scheduled workshops and training sessions to keep abreast of the latest information about marine mammals and the ocean environment. Attendance is considered part of their salaried responsibilities, so they are paid to learn. Promotion and salary increases are in part determined by the quality of participation in such events.

Pacific Whale Foundation employees who use public transportation to and from work are reimbursed for up to one-third of the travel cost. Employees who purchase a hybrid vehicle are also awarded a rebate. All staff members are invited to serve

Educational programs need to be developed according to the age and interests of the participants.

on a range of committees that help set company policies and procedures and plan new initiatives.

GUEST SERVICES:

Pacific Whale Foundation's onboard programs promote environmentally sound practices and provide guests with follow-up opportunities to actually put some of those practices to work. Education programs are developed in-house, based on research conducted by Pacific Whale Foundation scientists or in collaboration with researchers from other organizations. Pacific Whale Foundation naturalists are trained in the latest-available scientific information, as well as in the most effective interpretive techniques. Vessel design and program presentation ensure that all guests are able to hear, meet, and interact with naturalists throughout the excursion.

All vessel programs (dolphin, whale, and turtle watching; snorkeling; marine cultural history excursions; sunset cruises) demonstrate and promote environmentally sound practices. In collaboration with county and state agencies, Pacific Whale Foundation operates the Volunteers on Vacation program, which allows guests to spend part of their vacation time volunteering with any of a number of local environmental groups. These follow-up

Naturalist programs need to be informed by the latest and most accurate research findings.

Volunteer programs that reach out to visitors help extend the range of environmental education programs.

experiences help reinforce new behaviors that help protect the environment.

Pacific Whale Foundation is unique in developing a broad, holistic approach to marine tourism. It develops, tests, and improves educational programs. It doesn't just promote environmentally sound behaviors; it practices them every day. It excels in providing guests the opportunity to carry out environmentally appropriate actions through programs like "Volunteers on Vacation". The organization has daily access to and control of floating, real-life laboratories for experimenting with new approaches to environmentally sound marine tourism. With more than 150 employees, a fleet of modern vessels, and access to thousands of visitors each year, the foundation is also a significant part of the community and the local economy.

It has been neither easy nor inexpensive to put these practices into effect. Much of what passes for environmental education is empty platitude. Recommendations about how to present interpretive programs, regulations about how to operate around marine species, and advice on the best environmental practices often come from educators, scientists, government agencies, or nongovernmental organizations who have little or no appreciation for the logistical, personal, economic, or safety considerations of running a marine tourism business. By incorporating educators, scientists, and environmentalists into the enterprise, Pacific Whale Foundation is perhaps better positioned than most to provide effective programs for the public.

The fundamental lesson learned from nearly three decades of bringing humans and whales together is that experience matters. Operators, no matter how small or large, are in an ideal position to reshape the attitudes and behaviors of the millions of people they take out on the ocean each year. They need to be given more encouragement and resources to take advantage of that opportunity. Operators generally view their effort as a business enterprise first and foremost. The consequent drive to maximize short-term profit can threaten to overshadow long-term concern about the environment, and generate activities that lead those outside the industry to clamor for regulatory controls. An essential component of a credible ecotourism business is that it plays a significant role in benefiting the community—not just the customer, the target species, or the business's bottom line.

This has lead to a whole range of community-based programs funded by Pacific Whale Foundation. We collaborate with local schools to bring thousands of children each year out onto the ocean and into our state-of-the-art classrooms. In partnership with federal, state, and county agencies, we offer a whole host of public outreach programs and community events focusing on individual awareness about

We all recognize that environmentally aware kids are an important key to an environmentally sound future.

the environment. We collaborate with other nonprofits and educators to produce brochures, books, posters, fact sheets, and Web site materials that are used not only in Hawai'i but throughout the United States and as far away as Ecuador and Australia. We provide hands-on learning opportunities for kids, their parents, and senior citizens to directly experience natural settings of ecological importance and to help restore and protect them. We even provide naturalist training programs for other operators at home and abroad. We recognize that not all vessel operators can afford to direct their profits to such a wide range of activities. Pacific Whale Foundation has demonstrated, however, that it is possible for operators to work with researchers, educators, conservationists, and interested laypersons to become a critical part of the solution rather than continuing to be a part of the problem.

Why are we telling you all this? Because we firmly believe you can be a

Pacific Whale Foundation supports environmental education programs in sites around the world, such as this effort in Ecuador.

part of the solution as well. As described above, our mission is to model in every facet of our operation what we expect of our own employees as well as our supporters and guests. We hope that what you experience during an activity with Pacific Whale Foundation will directly

It is important that whalewatchers educate themselves about what constitutes a responsible whalewatch, and only support those companies who provide it.

influence your own daily actions. Our success will be measured not only by how you enjoyed your experience with us, but also by how much you reduce your "footprint," conserve energy and water, and respect the environment.

A second focus of our efforts is to make you a better consumer. A responsible and knowledgeable whalewatcher becomes an essential component in shaping the practices of operators in a wide range of settings. Our data shows that those who go on marine excursions do so a number of times in different locations. To ensure operators rise to the level of best practices, knowledgeable passengers have to demand it. Change occurs when change is demanded. We recommend the following:

1. Choose your trip carefully. Do your homework. We provide a list of appropriate guidelines below.
2. Let the captain or the naturalist know what you think of your experience. Immediate and effective feedback is a critical way to enact change. Nobody is perfect, but honest feedback can improve anyone's performance. If you like what's happened, say so. If you don't like what's happened, say so. You can also register any compliments

or concerns with local tourism authorities.

3. Spread the word. Word of mouth is the most powerful marketing tool available. Tell your friends. You can also go online to a number of sites, like www.tripadvisor.com or the operator's own Web site, and tell the world.
4. Remember that it is just as important to express what's good as what's bad.

Finally, it is our hope that when you go out into the marine environment on your own, you will practice what we have preached. Whether you go snorkeling, diving, recreational boating, or even walking along the beach, it is your responsibility to leave the environment in better shape than you found it.

Chapter 25

WHERE TO WATCH WHALES IN HAWAI'I

Whales are distributed fairly widely throughout all the main islands during the winter months, and commercial whalewatching trips can be found on Hawai'i Island, Maui, Lāna'i, Moloka'i, O'ahu, and Kaua'i. Whales can be observed near shore from almost any elevated lookout on any of the major islands. Usually the leeward (protected from prevailing winds) side of the major islands provide the best observation areas because the ocean conditions are better, and whales tend to congregate in the leeward areas more than the deep waters off the windward sides. During the peak of the whale season (January through March; the exact dates vary from year to year) an islandwide project for the public is hosted by the Hawaiian Islands Humpback Whale National Marine Sanctuary and the Pacific Whale Foundation. Volunteer observers gather at predetermined sites on the islands of O'ahu, Kaua'i, Hawai'i, Maui, and Kaho'olawe on designated days to count whales and record their behaviors. Some of the sites reporting significant sightings are listed by island.

In Hawai'i exciting whalewatches are generally possible within a short distance of the harbor, well in sight of land.

KAUA'I

1. Ahukini Landing
2. Crater Hill
3. Kapa'a Lookout
4. Kīlauea Lighthouse
5. Lumaha'i Lookout
6. Makawehi
7. Māhā'ulepū Halau
8. Makahū'ena Point
9. Ninini Point
10. Pacific Missile Range
11. Po'ipu ipū Beach Park
12. Port Allen Cemetery
13. Princeville
14. Wailmea Canyon Drive

O'AHU

15. Diamond Head
16. Hanauma Bay
17. Ka'ena Point
18. Kualoa Ranch
19. Lāna'i Lookout
20. Mā'ili Point
21. Makapu'u Point
22. Mokule'ia
23. Pauena Point
24. Shark's Cove
25. Spitting Caves

MAUI

26. Hāna
27. Honokōwai
28. Honolua
29. Ho'okipa
30. Kapalua

31. Kīhei Beach Parks
32. Kohakuloa
33. Launiupoko
34. Nākālele Point
35. Olowalu
36. Papawai (McGregor) Point
37. Pu'uōla'i

LĀNA'I

38. Shipwreck Beach
39. Keōmuku
40. Lāna'i Landing
41. Manēle Bay

MOLOKA'I

42. Kalaupapa
43. Kaunakahakai
44. Pūko'o

HAWAI'I

45. Hualālai Four Seasons
46. Ka Lae Park
47. Kahena Lookout
48. Kapa'a Beach Park
49. Keāhole OTEC (Ocean Thermal Energy Conversion) site
50. Keauhou
51. Lapakahi State Historical Park
52. Laupāhoehoe Lookout
53. Mile Marker 7
54. 'O'ōkala
55. Pu'ukōhola Heiau
56. 'Upolu Point

Chapter 26
HOW TO CHOOSE A WHALEWATCH

• Choose a departure point most convenient to your hotel or residence. Find out if it is accessible by public transport.

• Select an experienced and responsible tour operator. Consider the number of years in business, the number of passengers served, and the availability of recommendations by local residents, guidebooks, and online resources. Avoid operators who promise to "get you closer to the whales" than other companies. Such promises can only be kept at the expense of the whales. Under no circumstances is it appropriate (and in most cases it is illegal) to swim with or attempt to feed whales or dolphins.

• Find an operator with a commitment to protecting the ocean. A good operator uses biocompostable products, participates in recycling, uses alternative fuels, and pumps their waste into an onshore station, rather than dumping it in the ocean.

• Look for a comfortable, modern boat. Choose a stable vessel (catamarans tend to roll less than monohulls). While the more adventurous might prefer a rigid inflatable raft, they should be avoided if you are pregnant or have back problems.

• Choose a vessel with a Tier II diesel engine. These engines dramatically reduce emissions from marine diesels and have better fuel economy (for more information, see http://www.epa.gov/otaq/marine.htm). If you choose a vessel equipped with outboards, go with an operator that uses four-stroke engines. These are quieter, emit fewer emissions, and consume less oil and gas than conventional two-stroke outboard motors.

With patience and care, an exciting whalewatch is just a matter of time.

• While sailing may seem the most green, consider the fact that it can be difficult to maneuver around whales while under sail. All sailboats, like motor vessels, must cease approaching humpbacks outside one hundred yards. Our experience has been that once you are in the vicinity of whales, a sailboat becomes a power boat in that it must drop its sails and use its engines to maneuver.

• While small boats with seating close to the water provide good viewing during close encounters, larger, higher vessels offer better viewing at distance.

• Look for bathrooms, a shaded cabin area, and refreshment service. The best boats provide excellent viewing from all areas.

• Ask whether whale sightings are guaranteed. Will the operator let you go again at no charge if you fail to see whales during your cruise?

• Is there a knowledgeable naturalist on board? A good naturalist will have a background in marine biology or related a science, and formal training as a guide or interpreter.

• Is there additional specialized equipment such as a hydrophone (underwater microphone) to let you listen to the whale's songs, or underwater viewing ports or cameras? Note that in most areas, opportunities for underwater viewing are limited either by the turbidity of the water or regulations prohibiting close approach.

• Select an operator with a clear commitment to protecting whales and the marine environment. Inquire whether the vessel has prop guards or shielding or deflecting devices to protect whales from being "propped" or otherwise harmed should there be an accidental collision.

• Look for evidence that some portion of the operator's profits benefit significant conservation programs.

Increasing numbers of whales and the passage of time has seemed to make whales more curious and comfortable around boats that show patience and care.

Chapter 27
FREQUENTLY ASKED QUESTIONS

Q: HOW FAR DO YOU HAVE TO GO TO SEE WHALES?

A: Whales in Hawai'i tend to be found close to shore. Typically you don't have to travel by boat for more than ten or twenty minutes before you see humpback whales. We often see our first whales as we are leaving the harbor. The distance or time required changes throughout the season.

Q: WHAT ARE OUR CHANCES OF SEEING WHALES?

A: Hawai'i's whale season extends from November to May. During these months you have an excellent chance of seeing whales because there are so many within a relatively small area. Most operators, including Pacific Whale Foundation, guarantee you will see a whale or get another trip free.

Q: WHAT'S THE BEST TIME OF DAY TO SEE THE WHALES? WHEN ARE THEY MOST ACTIVE?

A: Based on our thirty years of experience with whalewatching and whale research, we've found that whales are active twenty-four hours a day. The ability to see whales is more dependent upon weather conditions and sea state than time of day.

Q: HOW CLOSE CAN WE GET TO WHALES?

A: Hawai'i has the benefit of having some of the very best whale protection laws in the world. Federal and state laws prevent approaches to whales closer than one hundred yards by any means, including boat, kayak, or even by surfers and swimmers. Of course, whales are wild animals operating in their natural environment and can approach us as they wish. It's not uncommon for whales to come up along beside a boat at rest, or even swim beneath it. These "whale muggings" are not against the law as long as it is the whale that approaches the boat and not the other way around. In fact, when a whale mugs a boat, the captain can't put the boat in gear and move away until the whale leaves.

Q: WHAT DOES A WHALEWATCH ENTAIL?

A: Most whalewatches in Hawai'i are two to three hours long. The best ones feature an expert naturalist knowledgeable about whale biology, research findings, and how to interpret the behaviors seen during the trip. Some operators offer special programs for kids, and others provide limited opportunities to either observe or participate in whale research. Freebies such as a whale poster, brochure, or photographs might be given out. Refreshments and snacks are usually provided at extra cost.

Q: WHAT SHOULD I PACK FOR MY WHALEWATCH CRUISE?

A: One of the pleasures of whalewatching in Hawai'i is that you don't need to bring much. A hat and polarized sunglasses are good to bring. Reef-safe sunscreen is highly recommended. Early morning or late afternoon whalewatches might require a sweatshirt or windbreaker. Binoculars are useful but not essential. Don't forget your camera (video or still). Be prepared for the possibility of getting wet from water over the bow of the boat, the blow of a nearby whale, or rain. A waterproof case for your equipment is recommended; we have improvised many times with large plastic garbage bags. Remember, "salt kills"— one drop of salt water in the working parts will destroy most cameras and electronic equipment.

Q: WILL I GET SEASICK?

A: If you are prone to motion sickness, a number of over-the-counter medications are available. Be sure to follow the instructions written on the label. Antiseasickness medications usually must be taken an hour before departure in order to be effective. Don't count on taking or purchasing medications to prevent seasickness on board the boat—it will almost certainly be too late to help you. For those experiencing only minor symptoms, on-the-spot treatments like Sea-Bands or crystallized ginger can help.

It helps to be well rested and relaxed before your trip. Have a light meal an hour or two beforehand and avoid eating greasy food while on board. Crackers, dry bread, or fruit (especially papaya) are good snack items. If you become thirsty, sip on carbonated beverages; avoid alcohol. Stand near the center of the vessel and keep your eyes trained on the horizon. The bow (front) of the vessel will have the roughest ride; the stern (rear) will provide a smoother ride, but may be less desired than the center of the vessel if there are exhaust fumes from the engines. Stay out in the open air but avoid too much direct sunshine. Do not go below decks, and refrain from going to the "head" (a ship's toilet) if you feel ill, since it is usually small and claustrophobic. Talk to your fellow whalewatchers to help take your mind off your queasy state. If all else fails, walk to the rear of the vessel, casually lean overboard, act like you are looking for tropical fish, and "heave to."

Even the most seasoned whalewatcher or sailor can become seasick. We recall a memorable whalewatch when the ocean was flat calm and the whales were performing superbly. Everyone on board was having a grand time except one elderly woman. Her husband, an experienced sailor, was comforting her while extolling the virtues of being a good sailor. Shortly, however, she began to "feed the fishes," which triggered a gag reflex on his part, and they were soon both retching in unison. Not only did he loose his pride overboard, but his dentures went as well!

Q: HOW CAN I SPOT A WHALE?

A: Start by sweeping your eyes back and forth across the ocean's surface in search of splashes. Large splashes are usually indicative of a humpback whale breaching or perhaps slapping its tail flukes or pectoral fins against the surface of the sea. Smaller splashes may indicate the presence of a group of dolphins, false killer whales, or pilot whales. Another trick is to watch for blows, which look like puffs of smoke. A blow is the by-product of the exhalation of a whale or dolphin. The rapid release of air from the animal's lungs atomizes moisture found around the blowholes and in the animal's respiratory system, creating the misty plume known as a blow.

Another favorite technique of Hawai'i's seasoned whalewatchers is to simply look for another boat that is sitting motionless in the water. Typically it has stopped to view a nearby whale or a group of dolphins!

When the whale you're watching dives below the surface, be patient. As an air-breathing mammal, it must eventually come to the surface to breathe. Adult humpbacks have been observed to stay submerged for as long as sixty minutes; the typical "down time" is eight to twelve minutes. Calves will surface more frequently, usually every three to five minutes.

Q: WILL WE SEE A BREACH?

A: On any given trip you have a 10 to 20 percent chance of seeing a breach. Whalewatching is a unique, exciting experience because you will be observing wild animals in their natural environment. Humpbacks come to Hawai'i to mate, give birth, and care for their young. These activities produce fascinating behaviors like singing, intense shoving and pushing by males competing for females, and gentle playful interactions between mothers and their calves. Unlike a zoo or an oceanarium, these are not trained animals that perform on cue. We cannot predict with a certainty whether you will see a breach or pec slap or hear a song or watch a whale quietly surface in the distance, but we do feel confident that if you go on a quality whalewatch, it will be rewarding experience.

Q: ARE HYDROPHONES IMPORTANT?

A: Hydrophones are sensitive underwater microphones that can be used to listen to the songs and social sounds of humpback whales, as well as sounds made by other marine life. Hydrophones should be used when the boat's engine and generator is turned off. It is helpful to play the sounds over the boat's public address system. When listening to sounds you will usually hear several whales singing in the area. The nice thing about a hydrophone is you do not have to worry about approaching a whale closely in order to hear it. In contrast the use of underwater cameras can sometimes result in pushing the approach limits in order to get a good view of the whale.

Q: I WANT TO TAKE PHOTOS, ANY ADVICE?

A: Capturing exciting images of whales takes a lot of time, a touch of intuition, and a good deal of luck. You should probably first consider if you really want to take photographs during your whalewatch. That may sound peculiar, but it is important to realize that a camera can actually get in the way of your whalewatching experience. When a whale breaches close to the boat, it may be more rewarding to just watch it roll in midair and crash back onto the ocean, rather than fumble with your camera while vainly attempting to remember all the procedures necessary for the camera's operation. Good photographs of whales can be taken with any type of camera, but for environmental reasons we recommend using a digital one. A 35mm single-lens reflex (SLR) will allow you to use a variety of lenses which are readily available and easily changed. We prefer to use a 70mm–300mm zoom lens on a boat. This allows us to photograph whales either close-up or at some distance without loss of quality due to shake or the boat's movement and vibration.

Whether you use a point-and-shoot digital camera or a sophisticated SLR, there are several basic rules to follow. Hold your camera steady. Make certain that the horizon line is level in your viewfinder. Slowly depress the shutter release. Never follow the whale through its movements while taking a picture as this will blur the image. Set your shutter speed for at least a five-hundredth of a second; this will freeze the movement of the whale, the vessel, the ocean, and your body. Filters can enhance your photographs. A UV or skylight filter can reduce the brightness of the sky and the water's glare with a minimal effect on shutter speed or aperture setting. A polarizing filter will greatly reduce glare and increase water penetration.

Always bring a spare digital memory card with you. It never fails that you will have the best whalewatching experience the day you run out of memory! To get fine photographs of whales you have to practice, which means taking a lot of bad pictures of whales before you develop your own technique. About one thousand pictures were taken for every good photograph published in this book.

If using a video camera, the same general rules for taking digital still photographs apply. Avoid excessive zooming in and out on the whales, as this will only serve to greatly accentuate the motion of the vessel. You shouldn't have to pass out seasick bags when showing your videos to your friends. Also, it is very important to know that you can severely damage a video camera (and your eyes) by filming directly into bright, glaring sunlight.

Q: WILL BINOCULARS HELP?

A: Binoculars can help bring you closer to the whales and provide more detailed observation of their behaviors. Binoculars come in a variety of sizes, weights, colors, and magnifications. We suggest an 8 x 40 or 7 x 50 wide-angle pair. Rubber-coated, waterproof binoculars are a bit more expensive, but withstand abuse from close encounters with boat decks, railings, doors, and other whalewatchers.

When purchasing binoculars try them out first and learn how to use them properly. To tell if a pair of prospective binoculars is right for you, focus the binoculars on an object about one hundred yards away. If at the end of one minute your eyes feel unstrained and you can hold the binoculars comfortably steady, they are probably right for you. Take care never to look into direct or bright sunlight with your binoculars!

Q: WHERE CAN I LEARN MORE ABOUT HAWAI'I'S HUMPBACKS?

A: There are a number of educational and research groups that have an interest in humpback whales in Hawai'i. The following groups provide additional information.

Pacific Whale Foundation (www.pacificwhale.org)
Maui Ocean Center (www.mauioceancenter.com)
Hawaiian Islands Humpback Whale Sanctuary (www.hawaiihumpbackwhale.noaa.gov)
Whale Trust (www.whaletrust.org)
Dolphin Institute (www.dolphininstitute.org)
The Whalesong Project (www.whalesong.net)
The Ocean Mammal Institute (www.oceanmammalinst.org)
Hawai'i Wildlife Fund www.wildhawaii.org
Hawaii Whale Research Foundation (www.hwrf.org)
The Center for Whale Studies (www.centerforwhalestudies.org)
Cetos Research Organization (www.cetosresearch.org)
Cascadia Research Collective (www.cascadiaresearch.org)
Hawai'i Marine Mammal Consortium (www.hmmc.org)

Chapter 28

HUMPBACKS ARE PROTECTED

All whales, dolphins, and seals are protected by NOAA Fisheries Service under the Marine Mammal Protection Act of 1972 (MMPA). In Hawai'i humpback whales, sperm whales, monk seals, and sea turtles are further protected by NOAA Fisheries Service under the Endangered Species Act of 1973 (ESA) and by the Hawai'i Department of Land and Natural Resources under Hawai'i State Law. NOAA's Hawaiian Islands Humpback Whale National Marine Sanctuary regulations provide additional protection for humpback whales and their habitat in Hawai'i.

Special federal regulations in Hawai'i prohibit approaching humpback whales (by any means) closer than one hundred yards (ninety meters) when on or in the water, and one thousand feet (three hundred meters) when operating an aircraft. These and other federal marine mammal and endangered species protection regulations apply to all ocean users, year-round, from zero to one hundred miles from shore throughout the Hawaiian Islands.

REPORTING INCIDENTS

• Violations: Report one-hundred-yard approach rule violations and other incidents of humpback whale harassment or disturbance to the NOAA Fisheries Office for Law Enforcement (24-hour enforcement hotline: 1-800-853-1964).

• Injuries: Report injured, entangled, or stranded whales; vessel-whale collisions; and other marine mammal health concerns to the NOAA Fisheries Service (24-hour marine mammal hotline: 1-888-256-9840).

Chapter 29
BE WHALE AWARE

We are in full support of the laws that have been passed to protect humpback whales, and in fact, we worked with many other concerned individuals in shaping the final versions. At the same time, from long experience, we know how difficult it is to implement the provisions of a legal document in the dynamic context that involves human, boat, ocean, and whale. As a result of our interactions with whalewatchers and the general public, discussions with sanctuary and other government officials, the insights of other researchers, and experience in a number of international settings, we have developed the following code of conduct suggesting best practices when in the presence of humpback whales. These are not meant to replace legislative regulations or serve as legal interpretations, but we do believe they are excellent, commonsense guidelines that will lead to a safe, enjoyable time for both the whale and the whalewatcher. We hope you will take these suggestions to heart and be "whale aware."

BEST PRACTICES & GUIDELINES FOR OPERATING WATERCRAFT AROUND HUMPBACK WHALES

1. **LOOK OUT WHEN WHALES ARE ABOUT:** From December to May always stay at your helm and post an observer to spot whales while underway.

2. **SLOW DOWN, WHALES AROUND:** Reduce speed to seventeen miles per hour (15 knots) or less in whale waters.

3. **SEE A BLOW, GO EXTRA SLOW:** Reduce your speed to seven miles per hour (6 knots) or less (no wake) within four hundred yards of a whale or dolphin group. Avoid abrupt course changes.

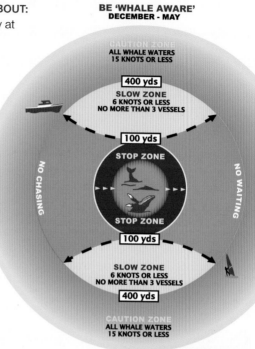

4. **BRAKE FOR WHALES: STOP YOUR PROP:** Federal regulations prohibit approaching humpback whales closer than one hundred yards.

5. If your vessel unexpectedly encounters humpback whales within one hundred yards, **STOP IMMEDIATELY** and allow the whales to pass.

6. **AVOID APPROACHING** whales and dolphins from the front or from directly behind. Always approach and depart from the side rear, moving in a direction parallel to the direction of the whales.

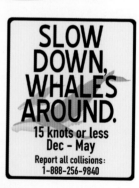

7. **KEEP CLEAR** of the whales' path: avoid positioning your vessel within four hundred yards of the path of traveling whales.

8. **BE CAUTIOUS AND COURTEOUS:** approach areas of known or suspected whale and dolphin activity with extreme caution. Look in all directions before planning your approach or departure.

9. **LIMIT YOUR VIEWING** with whale pods containing calves to thirty minutes. This will minimize the cumulative impact of additional vessels and give consideration to other viewers.

10. **MORE THAN THREE, FLEE:** Never more than three vessels of any size or type should stop to watch the same whale or dolphin group.

11. **DO NOT SWIM** with or feed whales or dolphins.

12. **DO NOT DRIVE** through groups of dolphins to entice them into bow riding.

13. Should dolphins choose to ride the bow wave of your vessel, maintain your heading and speed— **AVOID ANY SUDDEN** course change.

14. If a **COLLISION OCCURS**, immediately call the National Marine Fisheries Service Marine Mammal Stranding Hotline: 1-888-256-9840.

About Pacific Whale Foundation

I n 1980 Hawai'i's humpback whales were facing extinction. A young Greg Kaufman founded the nonprofit Pacific Whale Foundation, an organization devoted to saving whales and protecting their ocean home through research, conservation and education.

Today Pacific Whale Foundation is Hawai'i's oldest and largest marine conservation organization, with over a quarter century of proud accomplishments. Thousands of humpback whales have been individually photo-identified by our research teams working in Ecuador, Australia, Hawai'i, Japan, and other parts of the Pacific, providing valuable data on whale populations, migration, and social dynamics.

We have helped to establish protected areas for whales in Australia, Hawai'i, and Ecuador. We have fought to protect whales throughout the Pacific through legislation and education. We continue to identify serious problems that threaten whales and their habitat. These include LFA (low frequency active) sonar, marine debris, CO_2 dumping in Hawai'i, vessel collisions with whales, overfishing, and habitat loss. Recognizing that we can't protect whales if we don't protect their home, our research, conservation, and education efforts have expanded to include coral reefs, turtles, and toothed whales and dolphins.

Over three million people have learned about whales and the oceans through Pacific Whale Foundation's innovative ecotours, which promote eco-friendly interactions with the marine environment and teach stewardship of the ocean. Our Discovery Center on Maui serves ten thousand schoolchildren each year through our award-winning programs.

For more information, contact Pacific Whale Foundation.

PACIFIC WHALE
FOUNDATION

Pacific Whale Foundation
300 Māʻalaea Road, Suite 211
Wailuku, HI, USA 96793
1-800-WHALE-11 (800-942-5311)
www.pacificwhale.org
info@pacificwhale.org

Meet the Authors

Paul H. Forestell, Ph.D. is the provost at Long Island University's C. W. Post campus in New York. He was previously a professor of psychology at the same institution. He is also vice president and senior research associate of the Pacific Whale Foundation.

Born in Canada and educated at the University of New Brunswick, he received his Ph.D. from the University of Hawai'i in 1988. For thirty years Paul has studied the cognitive and social behaviors of whales and dolphins throughout the Pacific. He joined the Pacific Whale Foundation in 1981, and gained international recognition for his understanding of the rapidly expanding whale- and dolphin-watching industry, and development of formal training programs for naturalists and educators associated with marine tourism. In addition to aerial and boat-based observations of humpback whales in Hawai'i and Australia, Paul has conducted whalewatching workshops in Hawai'i, Australia, Japan, and Ecuador. He continues to study dolphins in Costa Rica, and humpback whales in Ecuador and Australia.

Gregory D. Kaufman is the founder and president of Pacific Whale Foundation. His efforts to protect whales began in the 1970s. Greg traveled throughout the United States and Europe, educating the public about the plight of endangered whales and demanding an end to commercial whaling. In 1975 he came to Hawai'i, the primary mating and calving area for humpback whales in the North Pacific, and began some of the first field studies of the behavior of live whales. A pioneer in noninvasive whale research, Greg founded Pacific Whale Foundation in 1980, and committed his new organization to educating the public, from a scientific perspective, about whales and their ocean habitat. Since then, Greg has proved himself to be a leader in addressing whale protection issues. He has pioneered responsible whale- and dolphin-watching programs throughout the Pacific and is widely acknowledged as an innovator and leader in marine ecotourism. Greg's work on humpback whales has taken him to every corner of the Pacific and has resulted in the most complete and extensive catalog of humpback whale tail fluke identification photographs in the Southern Hemisphere.

PHOTO CREDITS:

All images courtesy of Pacific Whale Foundation unless otherwise noted. Please note that photos used herein include images from research sites throughout the Pacific, including Hawai'i, Alaska, Mexico, Japan, Australia, New Zealand, American Samoa, Tonga, and Ecuador.

Monica and Michael Sweet: Pages back cover,14,15, 18, 44, 48, 57, 69, 78, 84, 115, 116, 118, 119, 121, 124, 127, 128 (top), 131, 144, 149, 152, 154, 156, 157, 164, 167, 172

Bryant Austin: Pages 55, 64, 65, 68, 70, 71, 72, 85, 102, 126, 166, 168

Special thanks to photos donated by Pacific Whale Foundation members and supporters:
Don Moses: Page 11 (bottom)
Cory Murdock: Pages 13, 75, 130 (middle), 194,197 (top)
Steve Dawson, PhD.: Pages 28, 40 (bottom)
Vincent Mounier, Page 32 (top)
Cristina Castro: Page 34
Steve Sonnenberg: Page 36 (top)
Jim Lustig: Pages 37, 67
Werner Van Steen: Pages 38, 93, 94
Carol and Herb Hartmann: Pages 62, 97 (bottom)
Bob Raimo: Page 79 (bottom)
Guillaume Blanchard/Punta Norte Orca Research: Page 96 (top)
Cheryl Sloan: Page 130 (top)
Debra Giusti: Pages 133 (bottom), 175 182
Dale Walsh: Pages 140, 141, 148, 173 (bottom)
Ken Held: Pages 142 (top), 143 (bottom), 146, 148, 151, 174 (top), 184 (bottom two images), 197, 200 (bottom)
Kristen Smart: Pages 147, 176, 177,
Leigh Catherine Clark: Page 160
Thomas Fake: Page 165 (top)
Carol Russell: Pages 173 (top), 214
Sarah Tobias: Page 174 (bottom)
Ros Butt: Page 183
Erik Voldengen: Page 199 (top)
Terry Taylor-Gingras: Page 205 (bottom)
Spencer Pendergrass: Page 206
Michael Beale: Page 212

ILLUSTRATION CREDITS:

Lilil Hagen: Pages 3*, 91*
Based on information by the Department of Commerce, National Marine Sanctuary Office: Pages 16, 17
Courtesy of Lahaina Printsellers: Page 19
Steve Dawson, PhD.: Pages 26*, 27*, 42*, 43*, 60*, 61*, 73*, 112*, 125*
Carl Buell, Page 30
Based on data provided in "SPLASH: Structure of Populations, Levels of Abundance and Status of Humpback Whales in the North Pacific", Cascadia Research, May 2008: Page 155
IHP Archive: Page 195

* Illustrations colorized by Helena Kim/Pacific Whale Foundation

We would like to make special mention of the contributions of our friends Monica and Michael Sweet. Their stunning photographs capture with artistry and drama the combination of the humpback whale's vibrant lifeforce and the Hawaiian Islands natural beauty. For more examples of their work, and information about purchasing their beautiful photographs, please visit www.pacificwhale.org/HOHbook